CHERYL CURRID'S GUIDE *to* BUSINESS TECHNOLOGY

Other VNR Business Technology/Communications Books. . . .

- **Designing TCP/IP Internetworks**
  by Geoff Bennett

- **Cases in Network Implementation: Enterprise Networking**
  by William E. Bracker, Jr. and Ray Sarch

- **Information Proficiency: The Key To The Information Age**
  by Thomas J. Buckholtz

- **Doing More Business on the Internet**
  by Mary J. Cronin

- **Currid's Guide to Business Technology**
  by Cheryl C. Currid

- **Networking Device Drivers**
  by Sanjay Dhawan

- **Routing in Today's Internetworks**
  by Mark Dickie

- **Spinning the Web: How To Provide Information On The Internet**
  by Andrew Ford

- **Digital Signal Processing in Communications**
  by Marvin E. Frerking

- **The Complete Cyberspace Reference and Directory**
  by Gilbert Held

- **Working With NetWare: For Network Supervisors and Users**
  by Gilbert Held

- **Global Expansion In The Information Age: Big Planet, Small World**
  by Thomas J. Howard

- **Online Marketing Handbook: How To Sell, Advertise, Publicize, and Promote Your Products and Services On the Internet and Commercial Online Systems**
  by Daniel S. Janal

- **Digital Telephony and Network Integration, 2nd Edition**
  by Bernhard E. Keiser and Eugene Strange

- **Internet Trainer's Guide**
  by Diane K. Kovacs

- **Low-Cost E-Mail With UUCP: Integrating UNIX, DOS, Windows and MAC**
  by Thomas Wm. Madron

- **The Illustrated Network Book: A Graphic Guide to Understanding Computer Networks**
  by Matthew G. Naugle

- **Making Telecommuting Happen: A Guide for Telemanagers and Telecommuters**
  by Jack M. Nilles

- **JPEG Still Image Data Compression Standard**
  by William B. Pennebaker and Joan L. Mitchell

- **Successful Reengineering: An Implementation Guide To Using Information Technology**
  by Daniel Petrozzo and John C. Stepper

- **Reducing the Cost of LAN Ownership: The Business of Running a Network**
  by Salvatore L. Salamone and Greg Gianforte

- **Using Wireless Communications in Business**
  by Andrew M. Seybold

- **Fax Power: High Leverage Business Communications**
  by Philip C. W. Sih

- **Applications for Distributed Systems and Network Management**
  by Kornel Terplan and Jill Huntington-Lee

- **SNMP Application Developer's Manual**
  by Robert L. Townsend

- **A Network of Objects: How To Lower Your Computing Cost and Improve Your Applications Delivery**
  by Thomas C. Tsai

- **Communications Standard Dictionary, 2nd Edition**
  by Martin H. Weik, DSc.

- **Enterprise Networking for Information Systems Professionals**
  by Norman Witkin

CHERYL CURRID'S GUIDE

to BUSINESS TECHNOLOGY

Cheryl Currid

VAN NOSTRAND REINHOLD
I(T)P™ A Division of International Thomson Publishing Inc.

New York • Albany • Bonn • Boston • Detroit • London • Madrid • Melbourne
Mexico City • Paris • San Francisco • Singapore • Tokyo • Toronto

TRADEMARKS
The words contained in this text which are believed to be trademarked, service marked, or otherwise to hold proprietary rights have been designated as such by use of intial capitalization. No attempt has been made to designate as trademarked or service marked any personal computer words or terms in which proprietary rights might exist. Inclusion, exclusion, or definition of a word or term is not intended to affect, or to express judgment upon, the validity of legal status of any proprietary right which may be claimed for a specific word or term.

Copyright © 1996 by Van Nostrand Reinhold

I(T)P™ A division of International Thomson Publishing, Inc.
The ITP logo is a trademark under license

Printed in the United States of America

For more information, contact:

Van Nostrand Reinhold
115 Fifth Avenue
New York, NY 10003

International Thomson Publishing GmbH
Königswinterer Strasse 418
53227 Bonn
Germany

International Thomson Publishing Europe
Berkshire House 168-173
High Holborn
London WCIV 7AA
England

International Thomson Publishing Asia
221 Henderson Road #05-10
Henderson Building
Singapore 0315

Thomas Nelson Australia
102 Dodds Street
South Melbourne, 3205
Victoria, Australia

International Thomson Publishing Japan
Hirakawacho Kyowa Building, 3F
2-2-1 Hirakawacho
Chiyoda-ku, 102 Tokyo
Japan

Nelson Canada
1120 Birchmount Road
Scarborough, Ontario
Canada M1K 5G4

International Thomson Editores
Campos Eliseos 385, Piso 7
Col. Polanco
11560 Mexico D.F. Mexico

All rights reserved. No part of this work covered by the copyright hereon may be reproduced or used in any form or by any means—graphic, electronic, or mechanical, including photocopying, recording, taping, or information storage and retrieval systems—without the written permission of the publisher.

1 2 3 4 5 6 7 8 9 10 QEBFF 01 00 99 98 97 96 95

Library of Congress Cataloging-in-Publication Data
Currid, Cheryl C.
    Cheryl Currid's guide to business technology / Cheryl Currid
        p.   cm.
    Includes bibliographical references and index.
    ISBN 0-442-02119-4
    1. Information technology—Management. 2. Information storage and
retrieval systems--Business. 3. Information superhighway.
I. Title.
HD30.2.C87   1995
658.4'038—dc20   95-40376
                                                                        CIP

To Olive B. Currid for all her inspiration.

Contents

Introduction

If you are like most business people today, you did not grow up thinking that you would have to become a computer geek. You chose your profession, studied hard, and learned your industry. Running a computer was for somebody else. . . or so you thought.

Then came the revolution. The PC was born, a few nerds and geeks found clever ways to use it, and before you knew what was happening, computer literacy became mandatory for career continuation. Computers are not computers now; they are information appliances.

Computers do not just compute anymore. They do a lot more, like help us arrange our words and thoughts, keep track of our things to do, store and share knowledge, and even *edutain* us. That is one of those new age words that somebody made up to explain that computers can be used both for education and entertainment. And, further it can be entertaining to be educated. Get it?

What is more, computers have not only changed everything about how we work, learn, or play, but they are changing all kinds of society rules. Of course, along the way nobody probably told you how to behave in this cyber-enhanced new world. Until now.

This book, hopefully the first of many, speaks to the issues of making computer and communications technology work for you. It is not a PHD book (push here dummy) and will not take you click by click through your spreadsheet or word processor. Instead, this book is focused (okay, fixated) on making technology work for you. It will tell you what technology works, for what occasions and circumstances, and how to use it.

Easy enough? I hope so.

Acknowledgments

Every book, whether it carries the name of one author or not, turns into a team effort. There are people behind the scenes to add a few thoughts, recommendations, and sometimes even serve to keep the author locked up until the manuscript is finished. This book is no exception.

My thanks must first go to my family who once again endured my crazy schedule during this project. My kids are somehow getting used to a mommy who beams in her files from cyberspace, then sometimes stays glued to the computer screen for hours on end. During this project, they too discovered the joys of cyberspace trekking through the teen chat areas of CompuServe and America Online.

I am indebted to Dorothy Wolf who spent the last six weeks of the project shuttling over work from the office, helping me handle moving into a new house, and keeping me locked up until I produced the manuscript. Dorothy has also served as inspiration to me, as I witnessed her transformation from a real techno-novice into a world class technology user.

Diane Bolin, now back for her ninth book (this woman must be crazy) took on an expanded role during this project. I let her loose with a couple of clipart packages and the permission to add a measure of humor—the results you will soon see. Her partners in crime were several software publishers who kindly contributed their software. T/Maker Company (415/962-0195) sent us their Incredible 25,000 Image Pak that does its name well. New Vision Technologies (613/727-8184) sent their excellent Presentation Task Force, that includes a gallery of 3500 clip art images and some of the funniest cartoons I have ever seen. It is a must for spicing up dry business presentations (if you have got the guts).

And, for the other team members at Currid & Company, Ram, Linda, Tony, Josh, Dianne D., and Paul who politely stepped back and did not chide me about the tough schedule for this project. It is great to work with such a dedicated, hard-working group who kept the company running while I worked through this project.

CHERYL CURRID'S GUIDE
to BUSINESS TECHNOLOGY

1

We're Heeeere!!!

Welcome to the electronic age! You are about to learn some of the most important lessons since kindergarten. This book is going to teach you how to survive and behave with business technology. It contains tips, techniques, and tidbits geared to turning you into a capable, fully functioning, electronically empowered business citizen.

Even if you profess to be a complete computer phobic, read on. You do not have to know a mouse from a modem to get started. I will take you through today's business technology piece by piece and give you both the basics as well as some little-known, yet easy-to-follow, advanced techniques for getting the best use of today's technology.

I know, neither your mother nor your kindergarten teacher taught you how to survive in this electronically empowered age. They did not know.

But, by now you have already figured out that you have to learn how to be an electronic citizen. Chances are that you have already found yourself surrounded by technology at nearly every turn. You know you are living in a very different world, with different rules and different attitudes about technology.

Like it or not, you cannot make a business move without using some form of electronic gizmo—a computer, cellular telephone, fax, or voice mail machine. And, chances are you did not grow up learning about all those gizmos and how they would invade your life.

Think about it. Many business cultures have already succumbed to parts of the electronic era. Corporate citizens talk to each other via voice mail, executives sport exotic pagers and cellular phones strapped to their sides, and many have adopted electronic mail (or e-mail) to pass bits of business information up, down, and

Figure 1.1. Electronic gizmos available today are making people more connected. With wireless phones, pagers, and portable computer's people are developing new work habits.

around the corporation. Business transactions have become both global and virtual—today it is perfectly acceptable to carry out business activity without ever having the principle players in the same place at the same time.

In the U.S., the computer and communications revolution has already affected most people in business; it is only a matter of time until the rest of the business world hooks up.

If you use a cellular phone, have an electronic mail box, or even use a plastic card to get money out of the bank, you have already been infiltrated by technology.

And, there is plenty more to come. Forget trying to stop it—for better or worse, electronic probes will find their way to virtually everyone in civilization by the end of this decade. With more than two billion microcontrollers produced each year, and ending up in everything from wrist watches to robots, few people can escape a modern life without some form of electronic assistance—like it or not.

Figure 1.2. If you use a cellular phone and an ATM card or even a credit card as money, you are already infiltrated by technology. And, once you start, you are hooked. There is no turning back.

Blame it on the computer nerds and geeks who started using computers to communicate and not just crunch numbers. Or, blame it on the communications industry that has made transcontinental communications links so crystal clear that you think you are talking with someone in the next office. Or, blame it on your parents—maybe it is just an accident of birth that you ended up on planet Earth at this moment.

But, whatever you do, do not try to stop the new technology from entering your space. If you have fashioned yourself as a technophobe—it is okay to get fearful or even mad for a moment—but then, get over it. Whether you like it or not, you are here in business today with more computing and communications gadgets and gizmos than any futurist could have ever dreamed of.

And, you cannot unplug yourself. There really is no turning back.

WHERE THIS BOOK WILL TAKE YOU

You can call this book a lot of things: your reference guide to the information highway; your driver's education; or your handbook for electronic etiquette. At first, you might even swear at it, but hopefully it will give you enough help with electronic gizmos that you will soon swear by it.

I have a personal mission for this book. I want to enlighten, empower, and help you enjoy technology. After spending the last two decades immersed in what information technology can do, I have come to learn that technology can indeed change a lot of rules about how we learn, work, or play.

Over the years, my technology consulting firm has developed a list of paradigm-busting technologies. The list, which changes from year to year, includes many of the new technologies that I will discuss in this book.

I want to share the secrets and some of the excitement about how you can tweak some of your personal and work habits to get a lot more benefits from technology. I designed the book to give you a little philosophy, a little history about technology, and a whole lot of practical tips to help you enjoy (or at least get more efficient) in the electronically enlightened age.

Over its pages, you will see how to survive and even become empowered by the electronic revolution. For the most part, I will focus on business, the office environment, and

Figure 1.3. Okay, here we go. Let me share a few secrets with you?

how to use technology for knowledge or white collar work—but do not let that stop your imagination. When you leave for home, you can expect to make use of your electronic skills there too. Today you can use your PC for education, enrichment, and even entertainment. In fact, a whole new industry is springing up that is geared to both educate as well as entertain you during your free time. It is called edutainment.

NO REST FROM THE REVOLUTION—EVEN AT HOME

Today you can learn how to drive a car, fly a plane, or become a speed reader with PC software. And, chances are, you will do a lot of this learning from the comfort of your home.

In the U.S., sales of home-bound PCs now exceed washing machines and rival those of televisions. In fact, the number of dollars spent on personal computers exceeded those spent on TV sets starting in 1994. And, with constantly plummeting PC prices and increases in power, you can count on wanting a new model almost every year.

The home computer market is big business (potentially even bigger than the office market). A study released by Computer Intelligence revealed that personal computers are becoming standard equipment for people of all income and socioeconomic levels. And, people spend a lot of time using their computers. Nearly 40 percent of seasoned PC users spent better than 20 hours each week tuned in. Some people believe that the PC could even replace the TV and the kid's Nintendo game. Don't laugh, PCs have a history of working themselves into the hearts and minds of people who use them. Look at office technology: During the 1980s, PCs replaced other devices, like dedicated word processors, fixed function terminals hooked to mainframe computers, cash registers, and limited function mini-computers.

A mid-1995 survey released by Lansing, Michigan-based EPIC-MRA showed that nearly 50 percent of American households own a computer. Moreover, 17 percent of those who did not planned to buy one within a year. For some individual neighborhoods that rate is much higher. Areas of Silicon Valley, California, Fairfax, Virginia, and Montgomery County, Maryland boast home computer penetration of 75 percent or more.

Of home computers, analysts estimate that a growing number will be linked up with global computer networks. During 1995, only 20 percent of home computers are used for dialing into networks, but the number is growing quickly. Survey after survey finds that Americans use home computers for personal finance, workday extenders, and the kid's schoolwork. But, there is decidedly more—education and entertainment are not far behind. That should not come as a big surprise. Computers are quickly becoming a consumer-oriented technology. And, consumers are adopting technologies at faster and faster rates. While it may have taken the telephone 20 years to reach its first million subscribers, it only took six years for the VCR, and four years for cellular phones.

Figure 1.4. Personal Computers are entering households as a standard appliance. As of 1995, half of U.S. homes had at least one PC.

An electronically empowered future is coming faster than most people imagine. Computer technology finds its way into just about everything we do. Micro-controllers, the chips that power everything from anti-locking brakes to kitchen blenders and toasters, have become so pervasive and invisible that most people do not even know when they are using them. Already, the typical U.S.

home has over 100 chips, and that will likely double or triple before 2005.

LIFESTYLE—WORKSTYLE: EVERYTHING CHANGES!

Remember George Jetson? He and his futuristic family were the subject of a long running cartoon series in the 1960s. The Jetsons used their air-mobile, space-styled vehicle to cruise between home, school, and work. They used wireless phones, programmable kitchens, video cameras, and other novel technology. Most viewers of the series were amused by the electronic capabilities of this mythical family but never dreamed that they would have to contend with an electronically empowered lifestyle.

Figure 1.5. OK, maybe you are not George Jetson, but someday soon, you may be flying between home, school, and business. Maybe not literally, but electronically.

Life does change in an electronically empowered world. For the most part, it brings convenience. Like my friend in Tokyo who lives in an apartment condo. He programs a keypad in his apartment to expect his arrival workday evenings about 6:00 P.M. Shortly before the appointed hour, the electronic drapes close, lights in the living room illuminate his art collection, the stereo starts, and his whirlpool bath tub fills with water warmed precisely to his desired temperature setting. When he opens the door, the environment is ready for him. Is this some kind of home of the future? No, he has been living there since 1992.

In my own house, I have a talking security system that conveniently lets me call it on the telephone. Aside

from the usual features of monitoring doors and windows, the system also reminds the family when a door has been left open or ajar. And, if a security sensor is tripped, the system not only sounds a piercing alarm and calls the authorities, its voice module shouts out

Figure 1.6. With today's technology, you can even secure your house with a touch-tone phone from anywhere.

"Intrusion! Intrusion! Sensor 21," and repeats itself until somebody turns off the alarm. Aside from security, the system features sensors on the thermostat and selected lights. I can call in from any touch-tone phone and adjust the temperature or switch on lights. Further, I can adjust the security levels for the house.

Other commonly available examples of technology conveniences paint a picture of things to come. Consider telephone technology, like Caller ID, caller return, and other options. Caller ID subscribers know who is calling even before picking up the phone. The service gives you time, date, calling party name, and phone number. It adds about $3.00 per month to your phone bill and requires a special phone or Caller ID display unit to decipher the calling name information. Some new home computers, such as the Compaq Presario, also come with Caller ID support so you can hook up your computer to track your incoming calls.

Workstyle Changes

The whole prospect of taking care of business is different today than even a few years ago. Low cost computing power—whether it is applied to your telephone, pager, computer, or wristwatch—has changed a lot of the rules.

When computers were expensive, people could not cost-justify using electronic gizmos for any purpose. But now, computers are cheap and people power is expensive.

The challenge for business people is to understand the dynamics of ever-changing technology. You need to learn when to jump in and try out new technology and when to wait for the next generation.

Simpler said than done. Today, many businesses are run by people who were not trained under the tutelage of George Jetson. Instead, many of us were brought into the business world by people that I call Ned and Nellie Neanderthal. These folks never saw a computer. They made up the rules of business during a different era. They created the 17-step sign-off procedure for a purchase order; the 21-person approval process for a salary increase; and the three-week loan approval process, even if the actual work takes only 90 minutes.

Figure 1.7. Many of today's business rules were made up by people who never saw or touched a computer.

An issue that confounds even the best of business people is that of trying to find the keys to unlock real benefits from information technology.

My experience tells me that technology can help in areas of efficiency and productivity, but there are more promising goals. Technology can help you invent whole new ways of doing business.

TECHNOLOGY CAN (AND DOES) CHANGE THE RULES

Society and business have only seen the tip of the iceberg when it comes to how technology will change the rules and possibilities. Here are a few examples:

Insta-Credit for Shoppers

Consider the innovative technology solution developed by Beneficial Finance Corporation for electronics retailer,

Best Buy. Instead of making credit-seeking customers stand in lines, fill out complicated application forms, and wait for credit approval, Best Buy began using interactive kiosks. Using low-cost video conferencing equipment, customers enter the kiosk and a credit specialist collects the information, electronically conducts a credit check, and issues a temporary credit card with the customer's picture on it. Time required: about five minutes.

Figure 1.8. Faster than a speeding shopping card, you can get your credit approved at Best Buy using video conferencing technology.

Aside from speeding up the credit approval process for customers, the system allows Best Buy and Beneficial Finance to align human resources more appropriately. Rather than staffing each store with credit specialists, the merchants can concentrate their best people in credit centers that may be located anywhere. Moreover, store personnel can go back to the jobs that they do best, concentrating on sales and making the shopping experience enjoyable.

If you are asking, what about consumer acceptance? Early results from Best Buy's pilot program showed that 80 percent of Best Buy customers readily accepted the new technology and used the kiosk instead of the credit department. "The customers loved it," exclaimed Christopher Steele, director of accounting operations for Best Buy Co., Inc.

Now, consider making a banking transaction in the same way. Banks, rather than staffing each branch with pneumatic tubes connected to teller stations, can place the tellers in a central location. Customers could drive up to an ATM-like machine, see a real person on the screen, and make sure the entire banking transaction goes as desired. The teller need not be physically located in the same location as the customer. In fact, depending on the limits of banking legislation (not technology) the teller need not even be in the same town, state, or time zone. Obviously, the technology gives rise to rearranging all kinds of work scenarios.

Smart Sprinkling

Consider the innovative thinking that emerged from city workers in Rancho Cucamonga, a sunbelt city east of Los

Angeles. Like other California locations, Rancho Cucamonga is faced with an arid climate, successive 100+ degree sun-baking days that can toast expensive landscaping, and all-too-infrequent rain. Water surely is a precious commodity that nobody, especially the city managers, wants to waste.

Figure 1.9. No matter what the weather, smart sprinklers can adjust themselves to properly water city property.

Simple mishaps, like keeping the sprinklers on during sporadic rains, or allowing malfunctioning sprinkler heads to flood areas, can dramatically affect the water supply. Likewise, a clogged sprinkler head that prevents proper irrigation could require expensive replanting.

Faced with increasing concerns about water conservation, Dave Blevins, director of Park Maintenance, and a team of people developed a workable albeit unconventional solution. Blevins enlisted the help of CALSENSE, a California-based company that specializes in irrigation control. CALSENSE makes equipment that measures water output from either sprinklers or other sources. The equipment transmits data about water flow to a central computer over phone lines. It can potentially save a municipality millions of gallons of water by letting city workers monitor water flow and stop overflow conditions.

While CALSENSE offered an interesting "smart sprinkling" solution, it did not resolve Rancho Cucamonga's problems. The town had miles of "greenbelts" (medians) that obviously lacked phone lines for modems. Ripping up the streets to install phone lines would have cost hundreds of thousands of taxpayer dollars and taken years to complete—simply not feasible.

Undaunted, the team enlisted help from a wireless data integration firm. Together they found a low-cost way to carry the data from the CALSENSE equipment to the main computer with Ericsson wireless radio modems, which operate over the RAM Mobile data network. Moreover, since RAM charges by the data packet, and the CALSENSE equipment transmits only short messages regarding sprinkler conditions, the cost of the wireless solution was minimal. The new system "polls" irrigation sites and reports back to the main computer. If there is too much water flowing indicating a sprinkler head might be broken off or not flowing, usually stemming from a clogged sprinkler head, a problem alert can be quickly routed to the maintenance department for repair.

The system not only helps monitor effective water flow, it gives city maintenance workers an extra set of eyes looking for any problems. And, it frees city workers from making unnecessary trips to inspect sprinklers. That saves the city more than just water, it saves labor hours, city maintenance trucks, and gas.

The Rancho Cucamonga team followed several practices of successful technology adoption. They encouraged out-of-the-box thinking, solicited outside expertise, and did not turn away from a solution that nobody had ever tried before. Moreover, in their effort to produce a more efficient method to monitor water flow, they created a solution spanning beyond their original objectives.

Great Gains for Grocers

Take a look at the technology-induced change that occurred at your corner grocery store over the past decade. Back in the not-too-distant past, the process of getting food on the shelves was both paper- and people-intensive. Sure, there were computers involved, but computing systems only solved parts of the puzzle for getting products on and off the shelves.

Figure 1.10. Grocers use of technology made the whole ordering, stocking, check out process go faster. Few of us would want to go back to the old days.

It took clerks with big thick order books at store level, buyers at headquarters, and large armies of people in-between. It seemed that products got from warehouses to the back doors of stores because all the people were standing end-to-end handing boxes down the line.

Then, when the products arrived at the store, things did not get much better. Each and every unit had to be taken from its case and individually marked with a price stamp or sticker and placed on the shelf.

And, woe was the job of the in-store clerks when weekly price changes came through. Get out the razors, peel off the old price label and affix the new one. It was another time-consuming task. At virtually every turn, both paper and people were running around in circles.

Then came a technology-induced change—the electronic checkout scanner. Instead of marking each and every grocery store item with a price, clerks needed only to run the item over an electronic reader that would recognize the item code, quickly look up its price in the store computer, and record it on the customer's receipt.

At first, this scanning system was expensive and not well accepted by consumers. An early adopter of the technology, Giant Food of Landover, Maryland, had to put on a large consumer awareness campaign in order to convince customers of the benefits that computer technology would bring to them. Soon the benefits were clear. The technology was such an incredible boon to grocery store operations, it more than paid for itself in short order.

The system's impact on grocers occurred in several ways. It affected the processes of pricing, checking out customers, inventory management, and reordering.

The first big benefit came from eliminating the need for marking each of the hundreds of thousands of items with a price. Then, it sped up the check-out process because the scanner could count the items on the grocery order faster than a clerk could by hand. Together, the pricing and scanning steps also eliminated human errors of clerks incorrectly price stamping goods or incorrectly ringing up wrong prices.

More benefits accrued. As the computer identified each product sold, it could make much more accurate records of item sales and reorder points. Instead of Mabel or Marvin making a guess about how many units of Crest toothpaste to order, the computer could precisely tell what past sales had been and more accurately forecast reorder points and quantities.

This new-fangled technology, which hit the first grocery stores as a novelty, quickly turned from a competitive advantage to a competitive necessity. Grocers who did not adopt the technology could not compete with their more efficient competitors. Profits were at stake.

Quick History—The Early Years

If you were not around or paying much attention to the microcomputer revolution in the 1970s, all the functions and features of new technology might come as a little surprise. Actually, today's technology was predictable. Let me give you a quick overview.

Much of the credit (or blame) for the electronic revolution can be placed on a young upstart group of engineers who formed an innovative little company in late 1968. Their big break came in October of 1969 when they landed a $60,000 deal from a Japanese company, Busicom, that was trying to make a better electronic calculator.

The mission: Produce an all-purpose programmable chip for electronic calculators. At the time, calculators required 12 different chips, each performing a specific function. Their mission was to combine the functions of separate chips into one. Busicom reasoned that smaller and less-expensive calculators could be built. Little did they know that they were funding development of technology that would fundamentally change everything.

In just nine months the "calculator" project culminated in birth of the microprocessor. Who was the upstart company who developed the chip? It was none other than venerable technology leader Intel.

At the time, nobody really knew the full significance of Intel's discovery. It took several years for people to understand how much the microprocessor would change the world. Luckily, Intel executives sensed that the technology could be used outside of the calculator business and struck a deal with Busicom to return the investment if Intel were granted the rights to sell microprocessors in other devices, except calculators. Smart move.

Within a few years, engineers and scientists began to experiment with different uses of the microprocessor chip. By 1974, now using Intel's third-generation chip, a hobbyist in New Mexico put together a contraption called the Altair, which turned into the world's first personal computer.

The race was on. Major developments and breakthroughs took place at a quick pace. There was a major milestone almost every year and minor miracles took place monthly.

Figure 1.11. Innovations came quickly in the early years, but many developments went unnoticed to ordinary business people. Only the nerds, geeks, and hobbyists knew the power that was emerging from silicon shops.

For most of the business world, these events occurred without notice. Few business people had more than a passing interest in the events that started to shape the future. An occasional story in the *Wall Street Journal* or a business weekly piqued interest, but for the most part the engineers of the early days kept the secrets to themselves.

But, the milestones quickly continued to mount for computing technology based on the simple idea of using a small programmable chip.

Since those early days, innovations have continued to come at a quick pace. You can watch the rapid progression of technology by looking at a number of indices.

While many people do not understand all the nuances of technology advancements, I believe that a simple glance at the progress in microprocessor technology is enough to convince anyone that big changes have already occurred, and more are on the horizon. As shown in Table 1.1, the pure horsepower of microprocessors has increased dramatically in short order. Both the number of transistors crammed onto the chips, and their MIPS rating (ability to process a million instructions per second) have grown exponentially in just the last dozen years. Even if you do not know what a MIPS is, or could not tell a transistor from a turnip, you are probably still impressed at how things have changed. You are probably also intrigued about what those changes really mean, and what they might be able to buy you. The answer is: lots.

Intro- duced	First Ship	Name	Transistors	MIPS Rating
1979	1981	8088	29,000	.3–.7
1982	1984	80286	134,000	1.2–2.6
1985	1986	80386	275,000	5–11.4
1989	1989	80486	1,200,000	13–41
1993	1993	Pentium	3,000,000	Over 112
1995	1995	P6	6,000,000*	Over 300*

Table 1.1. MIPS Ratings. (Source: Intel Corporation and Currid & Company.) * Estimated at the time of printing.

To equate the fantastic improvements in chip technology to any other field is difficult, maybe even impossible. A proud computer industry executive once quipped:

If the automobile industry had progressed as fast as the computer industry, we would all be driving Rolls Royce's that go a million miles an hour and cost 25 cents.

Aside from the processing power improvements, new more powerful computers based on the microprocessor chips are coming to market within months of the actual chip technology announcement. While it took computer hardware manufacturers over two years to bring the first personal computer to market, now introductions come within weeks or months. Not only is computer speed accelerating, but the time-to-market for new technology is too.

Other computer components, like memory and disk drives, printers, sound and video capabilities, have also seen dramatic price/performance improvements within just a few years. Computer memory prices alone have plummeted over 90 percent within the last few years.

The bottom line on technology is: big change. Price and performance curves have astounded all but the most optimistic industry analysts. They should continue to rapidly move forward at each twist of the technology crank.

For business people, this gives new opportunities to inexpensively capitalize on computer power. Smart companies and smart people will learn to harness themselves to the technology rocket and ride through the waves of change.

WARNING: TECHNOLOGY HAZARDS

While I am a big believer in the effectiveness of new information technology, I must confess that there is a dark side to it—especially if you buy the wrong technology or do not use it correctly.

Sometimes I think that technology should carry a warning label. Perhaps something like:

WARNING: IMPROPER USE OF THIS TECHNOLOGY CAN BE HAZARDOUS TO YOUR PRODUCTIVITY (if not your health).

Despite the impressive changes it can make, ill-timed and poorly installed technology yields pathetic results.

Technology Failures

Along with stunning successes, the technology industry has had its share of failures. Software and hardware makers sometimes introduce technology faster than many people can absorb. Some new products are arguably worthless. They come out as if they were designed by and for engineers—not real people.

Take for example, pen computing, which was all the rage in the early 1990s. Pundits, analysts, and technology vendors alike all sang the praises of this new technology. I remember one well-respected analyst climb out on a limb to proclaim that pen computing was the next big shift in the electronic age. She was convinced that pen computers would overtake desktop computers.

She predicted that people would simply throw away their keyboards and start writing on their pen-based tablets—pens were in and everything else was out. Right?

Well, it sounded like a great idea but 1990s pen computing products never evolved to the point where real people could use them the way she envisioned.

Pen-enabled personal computers of the day were expensive, bulky, and heavy. Nobody wanted to carry around a seven or eight pound computer with a funny looking pen (stylus) that was too easy to lose. Also, battery life on the early computers was limited to just a few hours. And worse, handwriting recognition software failed to accurately decipher most people's scribbles. Besides, most people can hunt and peck on a keyboard faster than they can write anyway. So pen computing failed. The over-hyped technology just did not deliver.

Therein is created a challenge. You cannot just go out and buy any technology; you need to sift through the offerings and buy what is right for you. When you do match up the right technology with the right ideas in business, you can start doing some very interesting things.

Putting It All Together

In many ways, I could sum up the discussion in this entire chapter with a single-syllable, six-letter word: *change*. And, computers do change everything. They are rapidly changing how we learn, work, and play.

As easy as it is to say, the word *change* does not always meet with cheers by those who must endure it. I have seen people struggle to avoid change in both business and technology, as well as people who revel in it.

In the chapters that follow, I will introduce some of the skills and philosophies you need to deal with technology-induced change. I will start with the broad skills then work into more specifics as I begin to discuss each technology. Remember as you read, my purpose is to help you become enlightened, empowered, and enjoy new technology. Have fun!

2

Getting
Started

What would you say if I told you that you wasted a full day every week? Would you argue or agree? Would you insist that you were really a very efficient person and did not waste time? Or, would you eagerly look for any tip that promised to put back a few hours on your clock.

If you are like most business people, you waste 20 to 25 percent of your time on what is called *administrivia*. It is the practice of moving piles of paper from one side of your desk to another, of attending meetings to plan your next plan, of writing memos, follow-up letters, and nonsensical status reports. If you are a *road warrior*, a professional that travels a lot in business, you might spend as much as one full month a year wheels up. And, since airplane travel is not very conducive to productive business activity, most of your up time turns into down time. Sound familiar?

You may be asking yourself, "How will technology solve this? Simply spitting out memos faster is not the answer. Part of the problem comes from corporate culture, and technology cannot change that."

Hold up, do not despair. I did not just land from Mars or crawl out from underneath a rock. I am talking from experience. I have seen many corporate environments transform once technology was correctly adapted to (and adopted by) an organization. Even the most stoic corporate cultures can change once benefits begin to appear.

A case in point: e-mail. Only a decade ago you could not get a self-respecting senior executive to approve even a low-cost pilot program for an e-mail system. I remember, first hand, being laughed out of a management meeting when I suggested a million-dollar investment in technology to support e-mail. The executives said, "What? why buy expensive computers when memo pads only cost $1.25." They just did not believe that e-mail could ever pay for itself. Most corporate chieftains were patently unwilling to invest a dime to prove the point.

Luckily some people looked beyond the immediate replacement of memo pads and found ways to pilot programs. Then, people learned that e-mail was not technology that would simply replace a written memo, instead it would allow people to communicate differently.

And, according to my research over the last four years, e-mail has unearthed some surprising benefits. E-mail makes it quick and easy to pop little bits of information around a company. It promotes short, direct, action-oriented communication. It also tends to violate command and control structures. It is just as easy to send an e-mail to the company president as the person in the office next door. And, best of all, e-mail cheats the clock. Neither you nor the party have to be in the same place at the same time to carry on a quick e-mail dialog.

In fact, it turns out that e-mail becomes the number one application for many executives. That is right, the people who shunned it the most in the late 1980s have become the most ardent users in the 1990s.

SURVIVAL SKILLS

This chapter begins to tell about surviving (and maybe even enjoying) electronic empowerment. It assumes that you might need a little help as you think through your personal work practices. So, at the risk of being politically incorrect or really insulting you, I will introduce our guide for this chapter, Cave Man Charlie. Charlie has the work habits of your average working stiff. Now, I am not suggesting that you have Neanderthal work habits, but old Charlie sure does. He has yet to figure out electronic empowerment or how to do his job better with technology.

Charlie relies on his quill (or pen) and reams of paper. When he wants to send out a memo, he writes it out long-hand and then gets a secretary to transcribe it. When he receives a memo, Charlie insists on making extra copies for files by person, by subject, and by project. He may be organized, but he sure is inefficient. Charlie needs help. But, where does he start?

Figure 2.1. Cave Man Charlie did not have the electronic tools available today. But, what if he did? How and what would he use?

For this chapter, you and Charlie will study basic survival skills for the electronic era. (I am sure he needs them more than you do.) Importantly, the chapter introduces four skills you and Charlie should develop. They are: TTTW, which stands for Type, Talk, Think, and Write.

Also, in this chapter, I present a personal challenge for you and Charlie. I will give you Currid's Ten Commandments for Changing Computing Habits. These are my favorite commonsense tips and techniques for using technology more efficiently. Whether you can adopt them all overnight is subject to your personal capacity to endure change. I cannot honestly tell you that I have got them all down pat. Take a look and see how much of a stretch they are for you, your personal habits, and your goals. Good luck as you try them.

PARTING WITH THE PAST

There is an old saying that goes something like this: *Computers change everything.* The saying is true.

Computer technology gives people new capabilities. It obsoletes old procedures, techniques, and habits. It also requires that people gain a few new skills—like better typing, writing, and speaking skills. It makes them get to the point faster, become more direct, and dispense with the unnecessary fluff of old-style business communication.

Sometimes, those behavior changes become the hard part for people to take. They resent not being able to do business the old-fashioned way with protocols and hierarchy. While old-style methods might be comfortable, they are not effective.

Remember the peace and quiet of a plain paper calendar? It was the place to scribble little notes, doodles, to do lists, and special appointments. Now, for many of us, that private paper diary has long given way to sophisticated computer scheduling systems where colleagues can electronically invade and rearrange our time.

What about another favorite pastime, writing little office notes and memos? We would keep a handy tablet of yellow ruled paper at our side—and just jot down notes and have someone else, either a secretary or steno pool, turn them into polished, business-perfect prose.

Well, for many of us, that has gone, too. It has given way to electronic mail that shoots out our thoughts and ideas like a missile, which—if we are not smart about using it—could cause about as much destruction as a missile.

Endangered Species for the Office

If you have not already started changing your own habits, let us offer an endangered species list. Take a look around your own office to see how many of these relics you still have and use:

- Paper (or leather-bound) desktop appointment book
- Paper pocket version of the same appointment book
- Paper secretary's version of the same appointment book
- Desktop calculator or adding machine
- Paper notepad
- Paper to-do list or notebook
- Telephone message slips that say "while you were out"
- Address and phone number book (paper version)

The computer and communications revolution are affecting everything in the office, like it or not. As time and technology move forward, there is no escaping the invasion of both our business or personal lives.

Skills You Will Need to Develop

All of this talk might make you a little queasy about surviving in a technology-pervasive world. To survive, much less capitalize on, the electronic era, I believe you need a set of well-developed mechanical, thinking, and communications skills. The critical ones will make you ready to become computer-literate, or enhance the literacy you already have. These skills include the ability to:

- Type
- Talk
- Think
- Write

Each one is important, and if you lack a well-developed skill in any one of the areas, I strongly encourage you to get an improvement program started. Here is the list:

Type

Despite some advances in voice recognition and pen-based computing, do not count on them as an excuse from typing class. I discussed the setback of pen computing in Chapter 1 and I doubt that anyone will develop greatly improved technology solutions this decade. I believe the primary way to get information into computers for the next decade will remain your 10 fingers on a keyboard. Sorry.

Figure 2.2. First, Cave Man Charlie needs to learn how to type.

It is time to find Henryetta Hornsbee, the high school typing teacher, and make amends. Over the years, I have watched professional people seriously impair their productivity because they lacked simple mechanical skills in typing. And, they often found that their brains could not function as well when they spent too much effort hunting and pecking around a keyboard.

Do not look for miracle solutions to appear. The simple fact is that handwriting recognition software is at best inaccurate. Although there are emerging technologies, like Graffiti, that have better strike rates at recognition, these will require you to learn how to write differently. Pen computers are fine for making check marks in boxes, or gestures, but they simply are not worth the effort for deciphering handwriting well.

You will better spend your time learning how to type than write in some awkward alphabet. Besides, even if handwriting recognition were better, most people can learn to type much faster than they write. Even a poor typist will ultimately get to speeds of 40–45 words per minute, while regular handwriting speeds usually get to less than 20 words per minute.

Voice recognition technology, as input into computers, is still far from perfect and remains costly. While simple commands can be trained into a computer, normal speech still eludes all but the most expensive systems.

My suggestion is simple: Learn how to type.

If you do not have good typing skills, you will find no better teacher than the computer itself. Several excellent tutorial software packages are available to teach keyboard skills. If you have bought yourself a computer with a CD-ROM drive, you may have received a copy of Mavis Bacon's excellent typing tutorial as one of the software packages bundled with the drive. Alternatively, check with your local software store for the latest in typing tutors.

Also, consider purchasing a newly styled ergonomic keyboard, such as the Microsoft Natural keyboard. These advanced designed keyboards do make it more comfortable to type, especially if you have a lot of work.

Talk

Whether you are calling a voice-mail system, or the phone in someone's pocket or purse, you better be prepared to talk. If you are not a trained extemporaneous speaker, you might want to get some help collecting your thoughts, preparing your prose, and speaking in a voice that is clear and easy (and maybe even pleasant) to understand.

Figure 2.3. Cave Man Charlie masters voice mail.

With each day, you will find yourself talking to voice-mail systems. These devices record your every "ah" and "uh" in painfully accurate detail. Or, if you do contact a person real time, he or she is likely to be busy or on the move with a cellular phone. It is important to have something to say, and say it clearly and succinctly. Garbled, unconnected thoughts spoken in a hushed or monotone voice are unlikely to win you any friends or influence the receiver of your message.

To learn how to talk in business today, you will have to practice. Buy yourself an inexpensive hand-held tape recorder and practice leaving messages. Also, before you make a call, jot down a note with the three or four important points of your message.

A little-known trick of professionals is to stand when you are talking. Take a couple of seconds before the conversation for deep breathing. You will get the full benefit of using your diaphragm and improve the tonal quality of your voice.

If you get stage fright when you hear the "beep" of an answering machine, practice leaving yourself messages on your own voice-mail system. Over time, you will learn how to create messages that are prepared and polished.

· Do not leave content-free messages. Be sure to say something other than "John, this is Harry, please call me back." It could mean the difference between someone wanting to do business with you or not. For more tips and suggestions about the fine art of talking in the electronic era, make sure you check out Chapter 5.

Think

Think before you act electronically. Remember, once you hit the send key, your electronic message goes and there

is no turning back. Whether it is voice mail, e-mail, or even a fax, SEND means send. Few computer systems offer an easy way to retract a hastily written memo.

The "thinking" skill you need to develop comes in two parts: the ability to pull appro-priate, logical facts together; and the ability to think calmly before firing off electronic re-sponses.

The first skill comes with time and experience. The elec-

Figure 2.4. Thinking re-quires logical facts and calm-ness. Even Cave Man Char-lie needs to practice a little or he will send a flame mail message.

tronic world's unfolding gives people access to vast amounts of data and information. If you have the right passwords, a little knowledge, a modem, and a PC, you can already get to most of the information on the planet. As time and in-formation highway systems are built, there will be more.

Many people will start to show signs of informa-tion overload. That is, they will overdose on information because they will not know how to think and filter their way through the good data, and skip the unnecessary and meaningless data.

A critical skill, therefore, is to nurture the ability to know and think through information sources: to determine what is important.

I propose a second thinking skill also. This is the skill that watches behavior. That is, think before you act.

Frequently, people do not think before they shoot off a response to a disturbing e-mail or voice-mail message—that is called "flaming." And, while people joke about getting "flame mail," few really like receiving it. In fact, it can cause more harm than good and the sender often gets burned.

Remember, just because you can answer an e-mail message in an instant, it does not mean you should. Sometimes discretion is called for. Consider these techniques for dealing with disturbing news. Pick from these options:

♦ Walk around your desk
♦ Take a few deep breaths and write a draft of your thoughts
♦ Get a cup of coffee
♦ Rearrange the knickknacks on your desk
♦ Only answer disturbing mail after lunch, on a full stomach
♦ Call in a colleague—get a second opinion before hitting the send key
♦ Make a few phone calls, then answer the message
♦ Answer it tomorrow (but send an acknowledgment that you received it)

Get the picture? Buy yourself some time before flaming back an answer that you will be sorry for and cannot erase. Try to diffuse your emotional circuits before you launch back an answer. (I will talk about special techniques for thinking through e-mail issues in Chapter 7 of this book. But, for now, remember, think before you hit that send key.)

Write

It has been said that the world belongs to good writers. In the electronic world, good, clear writing is one of the most

Figure 2.5. You must be able to think and type at the same time.

important skills you can develop. Good writing skills often require that you master two of the other skills, typing and thinking. If you can type and think at the same time, chances are that you are well on your way to becoming a good writer.

As work teams mutate into geographically (or even globally) disbursed organizations, you might find yourself with a situation where the only contact you have with your colleagues is through writing. In these situations, it becomes critical to master the fine art of putting down your thoughts in an order that people find easy to understand and digest.

The message is: Learn how to write short, pithy, action-oriented messages. Chances are, you will be sending them electronically, and over time you will develop a less formal, less verbose way to get your message across. I think you should develop that skill sooner, rather than later.

CURRID'S TEN COMMANDMENTS FOR COMPUTING

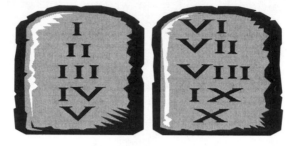

Surviving (and becoming empowered by) the electronic era will depend on your ability to use computers and communications technology effectively. In the beginning, it is no picnic. You probably have plenty of burned-in, time-honored, but time-wasting habits that are hard to change.

To help you get through some of the changes, here is a list of Currid's Top Ten techniques for forging new habits. If you can do them all, I guarantee you better productivity, peace, and eternal electronic happiness.

The list is:

1. Don't compute alone—demand a LAN.
2. Adorn your desk top—put your PC on it.
3. Crumple up your paper calendar.
4. Crush your calculator.
5. Nuke your note pads.
6. Tear up your "to do" lists.
7. Remove your Rolodex.
8. Make yourself multitask.
9. Wipe out your white board.
10. Refrain from recreating the wheel.

Sound easy? It is. Let's take each tip and talk about some techniques to make them your new habits.

1. Don't compute alone—demand a LAN

Unconnected personal computers, whether they are desktop units or mobile computers, are useless to a business

environment. All they do is create islands of information. The flow of information in the office will grind to a near halt because it is too hard to share. It is imperative to create a system where information, files, or work with co-workers and colleagues can be easily passed around.

Figure 2.6. Demand a LAN.

Without it, people start collecting redundant data files, they duplicate expensive resources (like laser printers), and waste tons of time walking diskettes around the office (or worse, re-key information from printed reports) when they want to share things.

So, tip number one is to get connected. In the office, every desktop computer should be hooked to some form of a network. That network can be a simple workgroup-based local area network (LAN) or a network that spans the globe. The network should be designed to not only hook computers together, but people too. For mobile computers, each and every one should have a modem so that you can at least dial back into the home office.

At a very minimum, the network should be set up with some form of e-mail and file sharing—so you can collaborate with colleagues even when you are not physically there. Make sure you have a place to put shared files, especially if you work on a team.

I also suggest that you load up the LAN with productivity-improving applications—not just a spreadsheet and word-processing software. All too often, people only learn one or two tools, then try to force fit every application to the tool. That causes the information equivalent of shoving a square peg into a round hole. It is not a good fit.

In addition to spreadsheets and word-processing software, LAN available applications should include: e-mail, graphics software, electronic calendars, database or filer software, work flow helpers, and communications abilities to outside networks and data banks. Depending on your particular job, you might also want to add project management, accounting, or other job-specific applications.

2. Adorn your desk top—put your PC on It

Your personal computer belongs on your desk, front and center. It does not matter what you have to move to get it

Figure 2.7. Place your computer directly on your desk. Make it easily accessible at all times.

there. Pictures of Aunt Martha or the kids can be relegated to credenzas or back bars; calculators, pen sets, and staplers can be shoved in drawers; and other assorted ornaments can be moved to the side.

The simple fact is, if you do not have your computer *within an arm's reach,* you will not use it as effectively. If your computer is directly in front of you, then you will find it much easier to use it for your every information need. If your furniture simply does not allow you to put everything in front of you, consider buying a small table, a pedestal, or some other type of stand. Also, measure the height of your keyboard. Most desks were designed for writing, not for computer keyboards. The desktop surface is usually three to four inches too high. Most people find a comfortable keyboard height at between 28" and 30". Desk top heights of 31" to 33" can cause a strain even for moderate amounts of keyboard activity.

What is important to remember is keeping that computer and keyboard close by. This tip goes a long way toward breaking old habits and making it easy to put things in your computer first, rather than on paper.

3. Crumple up your paper calendar

Paper calendars are passé. Especially for active business professionals who need to share scheduling information.

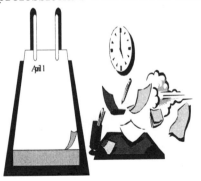

Figure 2.8. Get rid of that paper calendar.

Despite the comfort that many of us have gained over the years, there is nothing efficient about a paper calendar. No matter how hard you try to pass copies of your paper calendar around, you cannot beat the efficiency of the new electronic calendar and scheduling software available for LANs. Products like WordPerfect's Office, or Microsoft's Schedule+ will more than pay for themselves as they help business people create, share, and communicate appointment and meeting information.

Another benefit of getting everyone in the office up on scheduling software is to end "meeting madness." Some companies have administrative assistants and secretaries spend up to 40 percent of their time arranging meetings. Just pulling together a small group of four or five people could generate as many as 20 telephone calls and take several days. But, if everyone maintains his or her appointments with scheduling software, the process of pulling together a meeting can be reduced to a few minutes—and no telephone calls. The meeting coordinator need only to pull up the schedules of the attendees, then ask the software to search out the best time for a meeting. The software sends out a message requesting the meeting to each of the participants. The process becomes quite automatic—and painless.

4. Crush your calculator

Calculators become unnecessary on the computer-enhanced desktop. If you have only a few numbers to add, then it is easy enough to pull up the on-screen calculator available on most desktop software, such as Microsoft's

Figure 2.9. Crush that calculator.

Windows. If, however, you need to remember how you put the numbers together, you are better off quickly pulling up a spreadsheet, and saving out the file in case you want to use the information again.

Changing the calculator habit can save you plenty of time during the course of a year. Far too often, people will scribble out calculations of the same numbers over and over. A much more efficient way would be to put those numbers into a spreadsheet and update them when something changes. But, that efficiency will never happen if you keep the calculator on your desk.

5. Nuke your note pads

No matter how adorable your note paper is, get rid of it. In today's world of collaborative computing, little notes

Figure 2.10. Nuke those note pads!

are to be shared, not scattered all over your desk or stuck to your monitor or walls.

If you have pads of those little pink telephone message slips in your office, get rid of them too. Phone messages are much more efficiently handled when they are put through an e-mail system and not shoved under stacks of paper only to be lost for days or weeks.

A good electronic-mail system, or groupware software like Lotus Notes, will go a long way in helping you make note taking more efficient and actionable. Once your notes are entered into the computer, you will have them readily available to paste into e-mail, a word-processing document, or some other application. That will not happen if you maintain nasty note pad habits with paper.

6. Tear up your "to do" lists

Just like your note pads, trample and tear up your "to do" lists. Even if you happen to be a neat, well-organized person, a paper-based task list quickly gets out of sync— priorities change, projects get done, new ones come in.

Many scheduling software packages have excellent electronic versions of task lists— and they let you easily manage

Figure 2.11. Get rid of those "to do" lists.

priorities. For example, products like Microsoft's Schedule+ software lets you assign due dates, priorities, and project identifiers to each task. These capabilities go a long way in helping people better manage their time and efforts applied to a project.

7. Remove your Rolodex

A paper-oriented business card file, like a Rolodex, can be one of the worst productivity pirates in the office. While it might be nice to keep the colorful business cards of all your friends and acquaintances, it makes no sense from a productivity standpoint.

Figure 2.12. Get rid of the Rolodex on your desk.

Besides, chances are, if you hoard name, telephone number, and address information in your own personal paper-based system, then someone else in the office is going to have a hard time getting the information.

Trash the paper system and find a good, group-oriented, address book package. That way, you can easily share name and address information with colleagues without them having to go through the process of maintaining their own lists.

You will find other benefits to electronic address books too. If you need to send out special mailings, you can quickly assemble a list that can be merged with the letter.

8. Make yourself multitask

Most people are quite capable of doing multiple things at once, and so should our computers. People who master

Figure 2.13. Force yourself to multitask.

the fine art of multitasking often load up several software packages and then quickly flip between them.

For example, using an operating system like Microsoft Windows, you can load up your favorite spreadsheet, word processor, e-mail package, and scheduler each time your computer is started. Then you are ready to switch in between applications without a lot of hassle.

9. Wipe out your white board

Figure 2.14. Get the white board off your office wall.

White boards are fine for brainstorming and creating concepts, but they are no place for maintaining lists or keeping information that you might want to see again someday.

Look for software that lets you share notes, such as Lotus Notes or the shared clipboard feature (called Clip-Book) of Microsoft Windows for Workgroups. As with paper note pads and to do lists, putting tidbits of information into the computer gives you a much better chance of ever seeing the information again. Remember, white boards can be erased by the cleaning staff at night, computer note pads can be saved to disk.

10. Refrain from recreating the wheel

If you have followed the first nine tips, then this one is easy. You have already gotten yourself into the habit of entering information, tidbits of data, and to-do or task lists into the computer. Now, you are in a position to share with your co-workers and colleagues, without recreating the wheel, or the information.

Figure 2.15. Do not try to recreating the data or the information.

Make sure you become adept at importing and exporting files or using the cut, copy, and paste features of your favorite software packages. Remember, data should be available, accessible, and only entered into a computer once. Look for ways to make it efficient.

ENTERING THE ELECTRONIC ERA

You have now been through boot camp. I have talked about the philosophy—you know the basic skills of the electronically empowered. You know that the electronic era is with us and, in order to keep on top of business, you are going to have to both cope with and conquer it. There is no turning back.

The next chapter discusses how you can conquer each element of the electronic era. Stay tuned.

3

Basic Gear

You cannot begin to use technology effectively until you have the *right stuff*. No, I do not mean the heroism, honor, and bravery type of stuff made famous by the movie a few years ago. I am talking about the right computer stuff. It is imperative that you carefully choose your basic gear (or platform, in computerese).

Now, let us get down to what is important for most business people. This chapter goes from strategic to tactical. It opens with my suggestion for you to develop your organizational and personal vision about business technology. You might find the process of defining your needs a little awkward at first, but go ahead and try to give it a little cerebral time.

If you start to think about what technology can do for you—either at work, home, or during travel—you are bound to come up with some new uses. And, do not hesitate to develop a couple of crazy ideas. At the frenetic pace of technology development, crazy ideas can quickly become a reality.

Remember Dick Tracy? He was the mythical character who intrigued 1950's viewers by talking into his wrist watch? Or what about Maxwell Smart, of the 1970's TV series *Get Smart*, who talked into his communications device located in the heel of his shoe.

Today these technologies do not look so odd. Anyone can buy a portable cellular phone smaller than

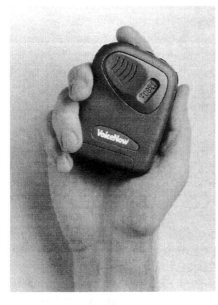

Maxwell Smart's shoe. Moreover, discount department and electronic stores started selling the Timex Datawatch, a wristwatch that your computer can program. In late 1995, PageNet and Motorola announce "VoiceNow," a pocket-sized answering machine/pager device that lets people receive messages with a caller's own voice.

My point: Do not be afraid to look beyond what you think technology can do for you today. Exciting new products emerge weekly. If you

Figure 3.1. Motorola's VoiceNow lets you carry your answering machine in the palm of your hand.

can dream it, there is a good chance that you can find technology to do it.

After you develop a strategic view of what computing can do for you, then it is time to create your shopping list. I will help you start that process by introducing basic technologies that will let you build a technology platform. Also, in later chapters, I will explore even more technologies, so do not put away that list.

Finally, I close this chapter with a word of caution. Since the balance of this book talks about technology—

piece by piece—I do not want to leave you with the idea that any one single piece provides the cure for your productivity problems. Despite accolades from people like me, technology alone will not resolve business problems. It will not cure acne or wrinkles either. But it sure can help you improve customer service, employee productivity, marketing and product research, and a host of other business activities. It can make you smarter because it can get to information that would otherwise be too difficult to get.

Now, if all this sounds confusing, do not be alarmed. Creating a tailored technology fit is not an easy process. Lots of people spend far too much money and time buying technology that fails to deliver. The problems come, in part, because people do not know how to set their expectations well. The tips, tricks, and techniques presented here and in the chapters to follow should help you gain a more realistic picture of how to get the most out of technology.

THE VISION THING

Okay, let's get philosophical for a minute. You need to develop a vision of what computing technology can do for you. In fact, I think you need to develop two visions: organizational and personal. You can develop these visions independent of each other but your best results will come when they merge.

Figure 3.2. Cave Man Charlie looking off in to the future.

From pagers, to cellular phones, to Internet newsgroups, you will find business technology at every turn. In fact, do not be surprised if you find it is easier to turn on than it is to turn off. Technology has permeated people's entire lifestyle and workstyle. It lets people explore new ways to do work, like telecommuting or setting up as an independent contractor and offering your services to many organizations instead of just one. It also lets companies rearrange work teams or reset a competitive environment.

Organizational Visions

When an organization deploys technology in a creative way, great things can happen. It frees up people to do things that they did not know they could do. It lets managers pick the best teams based on talent and not constraints like geography or availability. For example:

- Boeing tapped the global gene pool to create the innovative 777 aircraft. The company enlisted help from over 200 design teams that came from distant continents around the globe. Boeing brought together suppliers, customers and Boeing employees during the project. The team made heavy use of technology to stay connected. And, in the end, the team produced an exquisite product on time and on budget.

- Here on the ground, another innovative use of technology actually created a new business for Art Spinella's Oregon-based CNW Market Research. CNW provides measurements of consumer confidence and car transactions that are used by many auto makers and the Federal Research Board. The company is known for its ability to measure the elusive auto leasing market. This important part of the market has grown from 11 percent to 30 percent of new car deliveries in the last decade. Researchers cannot get good numbers from auto registrations because they list the leasing company as the owner of the car; and car companies themselves are reluctant to share individual information. Spinella figured that insurance companies know who is driving the car, so he devised a way to use those records to analyze the market.

Interestingly, Spinella does not operate this influential industry powerhouse from Detroit or New York, his office is located among the piney woods of southern Oregon—about 146 miles from an interstate highway. Spinella uses the information highway to collect survey information from around the continent and send the analyzed results to clients. His office: a converted cottage with a phone, fax, a couple of fully decked PCs, two satellite dishes, and a coffee pot. Two more satellite dishes adorn the roof of his adjacent house.

- Discount airliner Southwest Airlines turned a potential business threat into a financial advantage. In May of 1994, two of the airline industry's computerized reservation services booted Southwest off their systems because Southwest steadfastly refused to pay booking fees. Travel agents who used those systems began to encourage customers to call the airline directly rather than hand write a ticket. The phone and ticket writing burden swamped Southwest's direct reservation service. Rather than acquiesce, Southwest stepped up a plan for a new ticketless travel computer system modeled after a hotel check-in system. The new system gives the passenger a confirmation number instead of a ticket. If passengers need a receipt, it can be obtained at the gate. They piloted the new program and quickly rolled it out to system-wide availability. Within only a few months, 30 percent of Southwest's passengers were flying ticketless. That saved Southwest about $25 million a year. Moreover, it saved countless hours of back-office processing. Since most airline tickets are touched by 13 to 15 people in-between the reservations center to the final storage warehouse, cutting out tickets saved a lot of processing work.

The common theme to these examples: Technology changes jobs and activities. It can change the "who, when, where" components of how work gets done. Moreover, technology does not punch a time clock, wear a corporate ID badge, or carry a passport. But it wreaks havoc with status quo operating procedures. That, of course, is both good news and bad news.

The Personal Side

It is a good idea to align your technology vision with your own career and personal goals. Perhaps you aspire to be the foremost industry expert on plastic packaging. Or, maybe you want to be the best stock picker on the planet. Or, maybe you want to assemble a project team from the top experts of your industry to design and build a new product. Or, maybe you just want to pursue a personal interest and delve back into history and become an expert on the life and times of Ludwig von Beethoven.

Choose your goals, then set out to figure how technology tools can help you attain it. Trying to pursue some goals could lead you into trying new technology, like wireless e-mail or software agents.

What can you expect from technology? Consider these mission statements:

- Years ago Bill Gates, wunderkind leader of Microsoft, launched a concept of "information at your fingertips." In just four words, he transmitted a message of what computer technology could (or should) do for people. The message is simple, easy to understand, and a great goal for building out a computing environment.
- When planning the first local area networks at Coca-Cola Foods in the early 1980s, I encouraged my team to develop a vision of services that the network could ultimately provide. We figured that the company's knowledge workers needed a lot more than information about inventories and shipments. They needed competitive information, industry information, infor-

mation about changing government regulations, even weather information. For the desktop computers who accessed the network, my team created a sign-on screen that popped up the message "one-stop shopping for all your business information." That was it! Our vision was to deliver any information that anyone needed no matter where the information resided. Each morning everyone who logged onto the network was greeted with this message. It worked to encourage people to experiment and learn more about exactly what they could expect to find on the network. If a person could not find what he or she was looking for, we would find a way to connect the network to the right information source.

These statements set a personal expectation of what technology "should" provide. Your own vision statement should also set an expectation.

Once you set your own vision, then you should seek help getting the technology. If you work for a large corporation, you may have an information technology (IT) staff who will support your search. Or, you may find an outside technology consultant that you can retain.

A word of caution: Do not delegate all your technology selections and shopping to others. You must become personally involved if your technology is to fit properly. Like buying a suit, you will likely need some tailoring before the garment works for you. A technology shopper can do some of the legwork and search out what is available, but you must decide if it fits.

PICKING YOUR TOOL SET

You should start building your technology platform by picking out some basic information tools that will help obtain, store, and generate information. This requires that you first figure out "where" you want to receive most of your information.

As you think through your needs, you will no doubt realize that work is no longer a noun, it is a verb. In today's rich computer and communication society, work becomes an activity not a place. It becomes what you are doing, not where you are doing it. As a result, many people will set up more than one work location and try to look for ways to become productive while they are moving back and forth.

Most people want to set up their office with appropriate gear, but do not start and stop your planning with the selection of a simple PC and printer for your office. Consider other places where you would like to receive or generate information.

How about your home, your car, your summer vacation spot? If you travel a lot, will you want to have access to business or personal information during transit? If so, how will you get it?

Recently, I posed these questions to a series of busy executives. Of course, the answers were different for

each, but let me present a composite picture for a mythical executive that I will call Ed. Let's say that Ed is a busy executive with a company that manufacturers widgets. He travels a lot and needs to stay up to date on the activities of his competitors, customers, new government regulations concerning widgets, and a host of internal company information. Here is the technology shopping list that I would create for Ed:

Figure 3.3. Some of the tools you will need if you travel and need access to information at the office.

- **Office gear:** Even though Ed travels a lot, he still needs a high-powered PC for the office. It should be connected to the company's local area network. Further, his office should have high-quality color and black and white printers on the network, fax capability, a modem-sharing device so he can access online services. Technology makers such as Tektronix, Hewlett-Packard, Intel, and others offer an array of products to round out the office platform. We will discuss individual products later.

    The necessary software for Ed's basic productivity enhancement includes: e-mail; a shared calendar program so he and his staff can see each other's schedules; standard office productivity software, such as a spreadsheet, word processor, and a presentation graphics program; access to the company accounting and finance systems; several databases of industry information; a commercial online service for research, and access to the Internet.

    For group and project discussions, Ed should try out a groupware package, such as Lotus Notes. This type of software allows all members of a given team to share their ideas, notes, and progress reports.

    Since Ed works with team members in remote locations, I suggest that he purchase a desktop videoconferencing system. With low-cost equipment and high-speed data lines, he can stay in touch without leaving town.

- **Road ware:** For those times when Ed must travel, he needs appropriate gear for the "road warrior." This includes a color, portable notebook computer with sound capabilities. Standard additional equipment for the portable includes a high speed modem, remote software that lets him access his e-mail, calendar, groupware, and outside service (like CompuServe and the Internet).

Figure 3.4. Sony's MagicLink lets you maintain lots of information on a small computer. It also lets you communicate to and from a number of information services.

Optionally, he might want to carry a lightweight printer during some of his travel assignments. If he chooses not to carry a printer, yet needs to see a copy of his work, he can always fax a copy to himself at the hotel.

He should also carry a cellular phone and an alphanumeric pager that lets people send quick text notes as well as phone numbers. Cellular phones from Motorola, NEC, and Ericsson/GE all contain hands-free units so the phone can double as a car phone for around town.

Since Ed needs to stay "connected" when he travels, he should also invest in a PC personal digital assistant (PDA). If he is very keyboard-literate and wants a very small unit, he may enjoy the Hewlett-Packard 200LX. With the size and shape of a billfold wallet, it is easy to carry around. Or, if he would like more options and can spare a few ounces and inches, then he is a candidate for a product like Sony's MagicLink. (More about these items in Chapter 6.)

- **Home office equipment:** It is likely that Ed can get a lot of quiet work done from his home. If he is like most busy business people, he welcomes a couple of quiet hours at home when he can catch up on current events, write a few notes, or investigate a new idea. For those times, Ed needs a desktop PC at home that is configured much like his office. It should be powerful and have installed a full complement of communications and productivity software.

Ed may want to try and make his portable double as his home PC. That option works well for people who

Figure 3.5. Multifunction printer, fax, copier machine from Panasonic.

spend more time on the road than working at home. If so, he should invest in a docking station for the portable, and purchase a full size color monitor, separate keyboard, mouse, and low-cost printer. He might also consider buying a multifunction fax-printer-scanner-copier.

Next, let me turn the focus slightly. I want to talk more about organization infrastructure. Effective personal computing comes with effective organizational computing. If your office platform is a mess, than you will have a hard time achieving your potential. Here are some key features that you will want to make sure your office supports.

NETWORKING—FIRST STOP ON THE INFORMATION SUPERHIGHWAY

It is absolutely critical that a business organization—large or small—pursue a networked vision. This means you. Whether you are a sole proprietor working from your home, or an employee from a mega-corporation, you should not compute alone.

Just installing standalone computers will create nothing but problems in the long term. No one in business truly works in isolation. Everyone, no matter how remote and specialized the job, needs to connect with someone in (or outside) the organization.

Figure 3.6. No one in business truly works in isolation. Whether you work at home or in a large office building, you will need contact with other people.

In fact, I think you would be lucky to pick up any productivity at all with an office full of standalone computers. People end up working harder just trying to keep messages flowing and files synchronized through the office.

The networked part of the vision should be to connect all of the company's computers no matter where they exist. A good network computing strategy connects a lot more than the company's computers—it connects the company's people.

A computer network creates electronic paths so that people can collaborate across functional lines, geographic boundaries, and time zones.

Also, the design for the network must look beyond simply connecting up a workgroup, a department, a process team, or even an enterprise. It should allow for stops and access paths outside the organization and connect to suppliers, customers, research services, or any other interested party.

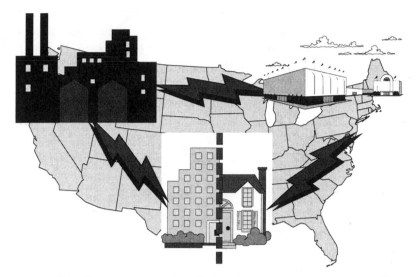

Figure 3.7. Your network should be able to connect to your office, your home office, your supplier, and your customer.

Technically, you can accomplish a connected environment by one of several means. You can hook up your company's local area network (LAN) to a wider private corporate network, or a public network, such as CompuServe or the Internet.

Today, much business can be transacted across public or private networks. The Internet, a public network, already spans the globe and provides a connection to over 30 million people. Private services, such as CompuServe, provide value-added services to over 133 countries and several million users worldwide.

BASIC TOOLS FOR YOU AND YOUR NETWORK

Even if your company has a network architecture in place, it is a good idea to review that architecture in light of technology's expanded role in the business organization.

This actual network infrastructure can often start with technology use for local area networks. It is not uncommon for companies to find that by placing all of the network computers on a simple topology base, such as Ethernet or Token Ring, a solid platform can be built. It turns out that these simple platforms work just fine to begin a company's global technology infrastructure for networking.

It is also very important to consider all possible ways for individuals to access the network. How are home users accommodated? What about people dialing in from hotels?

A Connection Checklist

Desktop computers and networks provide many flexible options—sometimes too many. It is easy to get hopelessly lost. Rather than list all the possible combinations of technologies, I am going to cut to the chase and provide a checklist of technology features you should have for your office environment.

Let me start with the infrastructure. Here is what you need to get connected:

1. A well planned and stable wiring architecture. Hopefully, your network wiring structure looks like your telephone wiring. All connections in a local building come back to a central point (or wiring closet). While other configurations are possible, it is far easier to manage your network when each location has a central area for network equipment.

2. Use of intelligent hubs and/or routers to connect and interconnect local networks.

3. A network operating system (NOS)—which is software that manages the communication on the network and certain services—like printing and file sharing.

4. Use of gateways to connect to the Internet or other services such as CompuServe. If your company has a mainframe computer, it too should be connected on the network.

5. Monitoring tools, utilities, and virus checkers. Today, there is a host of software diagnostic tools that help you make sure your network is operating at peak efficiency. Since networks have a tendency to grow beyond anyone's wildest expectations, it is important to have tools that monitor the effects of growth. They provide you with a warning system so you will know when to reconfigure or add extra devices before something comes crashing down.

6. Management tools to distribute software or check network devices, such as nodes, printers, and gateways.

7. Administration tools to help add, delete, change, or maintain network users.

Desktop Tools

It is important to plan your computing environment to be easy to use. Even if you are a very experienced computer user, you should look for shortcuts and efficiency tools where possible. Set a few goals for your desktop environment. At the least, choose products that support consistency, multitasking, and data sharing.

Software Tools

Software applications must be consistent. People (especially you) do not want to waste time learning which keys to push. In fact, nobody wants to spend time learning the mechanics of software at all.

A popular selection for the business office is to create a desktop environment based on Microsoft Windows desktop operating system. Windows provides a graphical user interface (GUI) that is consistent among different software products. A Windows-based word-processing program will have a good bit of consistency with a Windows-based spreadsheet. The same goes for a Windows-based e-mail package.

Multitasking is also important. Say, for example, you are working on a spreadsheet and the phone rings. Within an instant you want to check your calendar, add an appointment, then return to your spreadsheet. This type of task-switching is built into most Windows-based applications and provides a major advantage over older DOS-based applications that would require you to: save your spreadsheet file; exit the program; load the calendar program; update the records; save the calendar file; exit the program; then reload the spreadsheet program and bring up the worksheet.

Make sure your desktop tool selections also consider the need to share data. There are two approaches. First for each application you use, you should be able to share data created from one with another application that you use. Second, you should be able to easily share your data with someone else.

Often people want to add information they created in a spreadsheet into a report created by a word proces-

sor. Older DOS programs allowed this capability, but it was painful. It usually took a series of complex commands to save data out of one program and then put it into another. The process of exporting and importing data was sometimes so difficult that people avoided the pain by just rekeying the information they needed. Of course, that was time-consuming and error-prone.

Figure 3.8. Avoid the pain of having to rekey information.

For the most part, the Windows operating environment has solved data sharing among applications for individuals. Many Windows programs allow people to freely cut and paste (*embed*, in Windows speak) data.

More advanced Windows programs follow a convention called OLE (object linking and embedding, pronounced O-lay). This convention creates a live link between two or more applications. So, if you update a number on your spreadsheet and it is linked to your report in your word processing file, the number will automatically get updated.

The second consideration for data sharing is to find an easy way to share with others. If you are lucky enough to use the same application software as your colleagues, you can easily exchange files. If you use different software, such as Microsoft Word and Novell's WordPerfect, you may find it difficult to exchange files directly. Although many popular programs include file conversion utilities, they do not always work well.

Components of a Desktop Platform

When selecting your desktop toolset, make sure you choose basic tools. A good starting collection would include:

1. Spreadsheet
2. Word processor
3. Presentation graphics
4. Filing system (database or personal information manager)
5. Calendar
6. Electronic messaging
7. Access to external data

Some people prefer to purchase these basic tools from one vendor. Software suites, such as Microsoft Office; Lotus' SmartSuites, and Novell's Perfect Office, combine products into a single package. Buying a suite will not give you all the necessary desktop tools, but it will get you started.

Remember, it is important to look for software beyond the basics. Undoubtedly you will need utility and

specialty software, such as software for accounting, communications, personal information, and perhaps even "agent" software that will help search news services for you. For example, in 1995 Magee Enterprises, Inc., introduced Rosebud™, which is an automated software agent that collects news, stock quotes, weather, and e-mail information to send to your e-mail box, pager, or fax machine. The initial version of the $69 software pulls information from CompuServe and lets you set flags, such as a stock dropping by five points, or an announcement from a specific company.

Figure 3.9. Some of the software that will be required is utility, accounting, agents, and communications.

And, when considering utility software, do not forget two important categories: virus checking and backup utilities. Even if your network at work is monitored by a virus checker, you should check for viruses on your home PC and portable. Likewise, if you keep current versions of your status reports on your home PC's hard disk, it will not do you much good if somebody backs up your files only on the PC work.

Hardware Tools

You will find no shortage of innovative add-on devices for your home or office computer. Manufacturers have been busy over the past few years devising all kinds of nifty novelties from wireless pointing devices, to special graphics accelerators. This section focuses on three categories, printers, scanners and multifunction products.

Picking the Perfect Printer

No matter what you need for printing, you can find a printer that hooks up to a PC. Color? High resolution? Picture quality? Speed? You name it, you can find it.

The PC printer industry competes on two fronts, a beauty contest and a price war. Over the past decade

Figure 3.10. The printer business is part beauty contest, part price war. The winner is you! Prices continue to come down and quality goes up.

print quality has improved while prices plummeted. For example, my first really wonderful desktop printer was a Hewlett-Packard LaserJet that I purchased for my company in 1984. It cost $3,500, printed six pages a minute at 300 dpi (dots per inch) and weighed about 70 pounds. Today, you can buy a similar quality printer that weighs less than 20 pounds for $350 to $500.

For the office, I recommend that you follow a dual strategy of giving some people personal printers as well as a shared printer. Why? Some people generate a lot of paper and need the convenience of a deskside printer. Also, for security reasons, you do not want sensitive information like payroll records sitting out in a public printer. With laser or inkjet printers costing as little as a couple of hundred dollars, it is easy to cost justify putting one on many desks. Still, you will want to have at least one high-quality, high-speed printer for about every 20 to 30 people. High speed printers will set you back between $1,500 and $3,500 depending on features for black and white printing, or $5,000 to $7,000 for color.

Basic office printers fall into three technology categories: laser, ink jet, and dot matrix. For black and white printing, laser undoubtedly gives you the best quality and the most durable ink on the printed page.

Laser

My favorite printing technology for business correspondence is laser. It is crisp, durable, high quality, and available at prices as low as $350. (But, you will likely want to spend more, say $1,000, to get all the features you want.) Also, laser printers are whisper-silent so you can have one next to you churning out page after page while you are talking on the phone.

Pricing for laser printers is determined by speed, features, and resolution. If you are trying to economize, it is often best to compromise certain features rather than resolution. For example, the Hewlett-Packard LaserJet 5p costs less than $800 yet creates a page with excellent clarity.

Conversely, if you are buying a printer to share with others on the network, then you will want to look for a high speed rating, paper capacity, and fine resolution. For example, the Lexmark Optra LX prints up to 16 pages per minute at a resolution of 1200 dpi. It comes with a network port so it is easy to hook up directly to your network.

The following table provides a guide to selecting a laser printer that is right for your use:

Type of Use	Speed	Features	Resolution
Personal Uses	6 pages per minute (ppm) or more	200+ sheet paper tray, some internal fonts	300 dots per inch (dpi) for text-only printing, 600 DPI for text and graphics or photos
Office Uses	12 ppm or more (16–20 ppm for network printers)	200–500 sheet paper tray, multiple trays	600 dpi (although 1200 dpi gives crisper graphics and photos)

Table 3.1. Guide for selecting laser printers.

Inkjet

You can get low prices and acceptable performance and quality with inkjet printers. Inkjet technology is generally available at 300X300 or 360X360 dots per inch and many printers support grayscale, which helps with the resolution for photos or art.

Inkjet printers generally cost between $200 and $500, depending on features. Most print at speeds of three to six pages per minute and do not make a racket, like dot matrix printers do.

On the downsize, inkjet technology does not hold up as well as other printing technologies. If you spill coffee or water on your inkjet printed paper, the ink will smear—even if the ink has had ample time to dry. And, for my eyes, inkjet print does not have the crisp look of laser. Sure, the technology has come a long way in the past few years but (as an admitted print snob) I prefer laser.

Dot Matrix

Printers that use ribbons and a printhead to form characters across the page are often called "impact printers" or "dot matrix" printers. These printers are low cost and can be high speed.

The downsize to dot matrix printers is noise. They can make a racket and therefore make it difficult to talk on the phone or carry out other tasks while you are printing.

Color Printers

You can communicate a lot more than words when your business correspondence and presentations contain color. Documents printed in color can highlight words, phrases, or graphics vividly.

Many studies point to the fact that color has an impact on people. It helps draw attention, emphasize, prioritize, and even change moods. Moreover, the effects of color have been demonstrated to speed up the message. Think about it, if you get a letter or piece of advertising literature in the mail with certain areas color-highlighted, your eyes tend to zero in on those areas. Color printers can be effective office tools. (See Table 3.2 on page 66 for suggestions about what colors to use for your business communications.)

Up until recently, however, color printers were far too expensive for most individual or office budgets. Now, with technologies such as inkjet, phase change ink, and color laser, you can choose among many options for low price and performance.

For the cost conscious, it is hard to go wrong with color printing based on inkjet technology. For $275 to $800 you can buy a printer with at least 300X300 dpi resolution or more. Canon, Hewlett-Packard, and Panasonic, among others, make good quality color inkjet printers. Of course, you will have to compromise some quality and speed. Most printers in this category print at about only two pages per minute and do not print anywhere near photographic quality. They are fine for internal office use and some presentations that do not demand rich colors.

If you have a few more dollars to spend for a color printer for your office, consider one that uses laser or phase change ink technology. Both offer excellent color and can print on anything. For example, the Tektronix 340 color printer uses crayon-type, solid ink that it heats up and sprays across the paper. Then it quickly rolls the ink into place and dries it.

Figure 3.11. With the Tektronix 340, your office can produce high-quality print that rivals a professional printer.

Color Communicates

If you decide to get serious about color printing, let me suggest that you read up on uses of color for business materials. Many of the color printer makers have white papers with suggestions about the appropriate use of color.

You should keep in mind that the meaning and purpose of using color change from one type of audience to another. Consider the color blue. To some people blue means sweet, others think of it as a conservative "corporate" color. For people in the financial profession, blue means reliability, authority, respect, and loyalty. Conversely, to people in the medical field, blue means death. The shade of a color counts too. Dark blue, for instance, communicates a sense of stability, maturity, and calmness. Light blue is often construed as youthful, masculine, or cool.

To give you a sense of what color communicates to different audiences, consider the follow table:

Color Hue	Financial Manager	Health Care Worker	Control Engineer	Movie Audience
Blue	Corporate, reliable	Dead	Cold, water	Tender, gentle
Cyan	Cool, subdued	Deprived of oxygen	Steam	Leisurely
Green	Profitable, go forward	Infected, bilious	Normal, safe	Playful
Yellow	Important, highlight item	Jaundiced	Caution, impending problem	Happy
Red	Unprofitable, negative attention	Healthy, well	Danger, impending problem	Exciting

Table 3.2. How colors affect your audience.

Multifunction Products

There is an old joke in the computer business that says the only multiple function technology to ever make it big was the clock radio. That joke might need to be rewritten.

Starting in late 1994, manufacturers like Canon, Hewlett-Packard, Lexmark, Panasonic, and a host of others began to introduce a single unit that combined several office devices into one. Given the unglamorous names like "multi-function product" or "combo-unit," these devices combine the functions of a printer, fax machine, scanner, and copier. And, they do not cost much more than a printer.

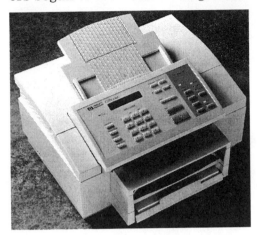

Figure 3.12. The Hewlett-Packard OfficeJet product is an all-in-one product that lets you fax, copy, print, and scan documents.

With them you can scan, fax, print and copy without wasting time running down the hall. They can save you hours (and miles of walking down corridors) when you want to send or receive faxes, scan in a logo, or get a copy. These combo units come with all the necessary software for the Windows environment. (In fact, some of them do not offer the high-end features for DOS-only computers. Yet another reason to move to Windows.)

During installation, they will set themselves up as a printer and a fax device. Also, they will answer the phone (as a fax machine) even while you are working on another task.

Most combo units are based on inkjet technology so they offer plain paper fax (which is good news) but less than perfect print quality (that is the bad news). They offer an array of features that you would expect from a well-integrated piece of office equipment. Still, for convenience printing and copying they are a boon to the office user who is innocently located far from the shared printer or copier. And, of course, these units are wonderful for the home office. Taking up the desk space of only a small printer, you can get several office devices rolled into one.

Scanners

Scanners let you take a paper or picture and copy it into your computer. People use scanners to collect everything from business cards to logos, articles to canceled checks. All scanners initially scan a document or picture as an image. In order to take a document and convert it to text, you will also have to use special OCR (optical character recognition) software. This software interprets the images on the page, and with 99-percent accuracy, converts it. Frequently, OCR software is bundled with scanners and, recently, makers of scanners have improved the OCR capability so the conversion occurs instantly without a second step on your part.

Like other office technologies, scanning has come down in price over the last few years. The options for scanners give you an array of functions (and prices). To introduce the options, I have divided up scanners into four categories: hand scanners, special use small scanners, page scanners, and production scanners. Depending on your needs, you may want to select more than one type.

- **Hand scanners:** If you need only to capture a quick logo, an occasional photo, or a few words of text from an article, then you will find hand scanners the way to go. They provide a low cost ($100–300) solution for quickly capturing information. You can buy units that scan in color, black and white, or both. Some come with OCR (optical character recognition) software.

  If you need high-quality color scanning, you will want to look for a product that scans in 800 to 1200 dpi in 24-bit true color. That will allow you to scan up to 16.8 million colors, which will capture the true colors in photos. (If your scanner only supports 256 colors, you will see a grainy look to the image.) Ideally, the scanner will also come packaged with software that lets you adjust or enhance colors or crop the image. So if Mable has a great photo of herself and Marvin, she can scan it in, crop out Marvin, and send it to Mel. Finally, if you want the best results with a hand scanner, it helps to get one that is motorized. Hand scanning can be tricky, one false move of the hand and you will distort and skew the image. With a motorized scanner, it travels in a straight direction at its own pace. It makes it much easier for scanning.

- **Special use small scanners:** If you have more than just a passing need for a small scanner, consider one of the special use products. For example, you can get a scanner that is designed to scan in photos, such as the Primax.

For picking up lines of data, a new type of hand scanner is emerging for text uses. Pioneered by Primax's introduction of the DataPen, you can use the device to read in lines of text directly to your word processing, spreadsheet, database, or other software.

Figure 3.13. Primax's DataPen uses a one-pass scan then OCR approach, so it reads in text to almost any software instantly.

This innovative device can save you plenty of time over a page or hand scanner, which reads in too much information at one time.

For example, if you were trying to add data such as an address listing to a database and only had a printed copy of the data, normally you would have to rekey each field of data. The DataPen can read and type in the information at least 10 times as fast as the most accomplished typist. It converts the scanned information to text instantly, so there is no additional processing required.

- **Page scanners:** If you want to capture documents, then you should look at page scanners. A page scanner can be either flatbed, which is great for scanning books, or roller fed, which takes one page at a time and scans it. These scanners are best when you want to work with whole pages of information.

Some come with innovative software that lets you easily work with the scanned image. For example, the PaperPort by Visioneer lets you scan an image directly onto your screen, then its software lets you drag and drop the image on a number of icons, as shown below.

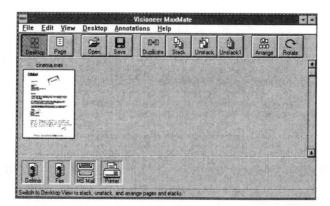

Figure 3.14. Paperport from Visioneer lets you scan your document or image directly onto your screen.

With this software, you can select the document and drag it to the fax icon to fax it to someone, to the printer to print it, or to the e-mail icon to attach it to an e-mail message.

- **Production scanners:** If you have production scanning needs, such as to scan long articles, books, or cleared checks, then consider a production scanner. The units, usually costing $5,000 to $10,000, let you scan in pages quickly. For example, the Panasonic KV-SP500 Series features two models, each with a 40-page-per-minute scanner, built-in laser quality printer, and either simplex or single-pass duplex capabilities. They support a wide range of paper sizes from business card to legal and let you scan from originals printed on anything from onion skin to card stock weight papers.

A WORD ABOUT HARDWARE AND QUALITY COMPONENTS

Before I leave this chapter, I want to make a few comments about how you should select computer technology. There is one simple, constant rule for choosing your basic computer equipment: Buy the best you can afford. Sure you can save a few dollars here and there if you buy no-name components. But chances are you will pay extra in the long run when the modem does not work with that discount mouse that takes a special driver to work with the monitor.

If matching up all the pieces and parts sounds confusing to you, then stop right now and vow never to do your own computer component integration. Unless you are an expert, you will spend hours with equipment that does not work well together. That is not a threat, it is a promise.

Also, proper hardware selection is often not stressed enough in business books. Several years ago, it was a popular notion for technology buyers to purchase inexpensive, no-name personal computers on the belief that PCs had become a commodity.

The penalty for saving a few dollars on the purchase order was often severe. No-name PCs turned out to be the leading cause of network glitches. In some of my company's research, we have seen that 20 percent of the computers have caused 80 percent of the service calls. And, guess what—those pesky problems were mostly caused by the no-name computer that somebody wanted to save a few dollars buying.

Since all computers are *not* created equal, users found that certain programs and applications did not run exactly the same on some computers versus others. Inconsistencies created trouble calls, network down time, and general dissatisfaction with technology. Some companies have learned that the cost of "cheap" computers actually ended up costing more in support and labor than the savings achieved over brand name computers.

Another argument can be made for selecting a brand name hardware vendor. That is R&D. Most major hardware and software companies have development arrangements so that new types of software are tested with hardware and inconsistencies are spotted before products ever see the general market. The time and energy to integrate and optimize hardware and software configurations are borne by the vendors and not the end user.

HIRE A TECHNOLOGY SHOPPER

You can build a very robust network and infrastructure without spending a lot of money. Somebody in the organization, however, needs to get smart about technology options and take charge of the technology shopping list. In large companies this role has historically been undertaken by professional information services (IS) personnel. In mid-sized and small companies, the role generally gets delegated to the first person who learns how to spell computer acronyms.

It is also a good idea to team up with a professional technology shopper. Consulting firms, systems integra-
tors, and some computer resellers often offer services to
help companies understand what is available with new
technology.

MOVING FORWARD

Infrastructure technologies are important building blocks
because they provide a solid base for other, more tailored
technologies. You would not think of building your dream
house with cardboard walls, and you should not build
your office technology environment without sturdy components.

Although you can indeed start building your business technology platform without fixing the infrastructure, I strongly encourage you to set aside some time and
effort to make sure you have got your infrastructure
technologies firmly in place.

Next, I will explore some key technologies, piece
by piece. The next chapters will address important technology and how to use them effectively. You will learn
some new tricks, and probably see some old ones with a
twist. The goal is to save you time, steps, and aggravation
of working with technology.

4

Facing Fax

Fax technology was introduced in 1924. It did not set the world on fire. In fact, it spent over 60 years on the market as a rich company's novelty. Fax machines were very expensive, fax paper was scarce, and people were concerned about the cost of sending images over long distance telephone lines.

The real promise of fax was (and still is) immediacy—not productivity. Initial uses of the technology caused more trouble than the technology was worth. Since fax machines were rare, you could only fax to people who had fax machines (a small universe). Moreover, because the equipment was expensive and specialized companies developed procedures and controls—often so structured that the process negated any positive effect of fax's faster transmission speed. In many large organizations, real people were not allowed to use a fax—only specially trained fax operators. The process of receiving a fax and routing it to someone in the company involved too many steps.

Frequently, incoming faxes had to be logged, sorted by the fax operator, hand addressed, and then sent to the company mail room where it would be delivered when the mail clerk got around to it. In other words, it could take one to three days to route it through the company once it hit the company fax paper.

In the early 1980s, things began to change. Low-cost, low-technology, easy-to-use fax machines were introduced. They were an overnight success. Also, fax paper became readily available at office supply stores, and people began to forget some of their initial concerns about long distance charges. Quickly, fax seemed to go from frightful to free.

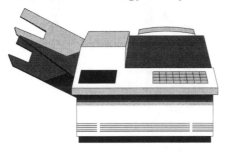

Figure 4.1. After 60 years on the market, once costs came down, faxes were an overnight success.

More importantly, "fax control" went out of control. Since new generation fax machines became so cheap to buy and easy to use, people started buying them and putting them everywhere. As everyday people became fax-literate, there was no need for a specially trained fax operator (so much for job security!).

Starting in the mid-1980s, a fax machine became the "in" thing to have. Now, everyone but everyone—from the corporate tower to the pizza parlor—has a fax. People started posting their fax numbers on business cards, company stationery, and advertising literature. Having a fax number is more than a status symbol, it is considered a necessity to do business. Fax threatens to make regular mail and some package delivery services obsolete for many (but not all) business uses.

In fact, for some people, fax might have become *too* cool. As a technology (and a cultural movement) fax has

changed colors. Some people have become fax addicts. They would rather send a fax than pick up a telephone or send a regular letter. I can defend this practice (sometimes) since certain types of information like lists, details, and numbers are more precisely handled by the written or printed form than the spoken word.

Figure 4.2. Some people have become fax addicts.

Also, in some situations, fax is used as a "poor man's" replacement for computer applications like e-mail, automated purchase-order systems, long distance telephone conversations, and sometimes solicitation. Some people use fax as an excuse for other forms of communication or to smother recipients with unneeded information (that is called fax abuse).

This chapter outlines the finer points of fax—and how to get the most out of it without falling into the fax-abuse trap. Call it "Fax Etiquette" if you must. This chapter covers topics ranging from fax philosophy to techniques of sending and receiving fax messages. It even explores fax technology options and discusses the advantages and disadvantages of PC and printer fax units.

STANDARD FAX FARE: SENDING AND RECEIVING

With the variety of today's fax equipment—from dedicated fax machines to modems with fax capability to multi-function fax-scanner-printer units—sending and receiving information could not be easier. No matter what type of fax machine you use, there are a few basic standards that you should follow.

Sending Faxes

Sending a fax can be almost as easy as using a copy machine or printing to a PC printer. Just press the right set of keys and you are on your way. Only, for sending the fax, you will have to remember to address the document.

Formal Fax Required   Informal Fax Acceptable

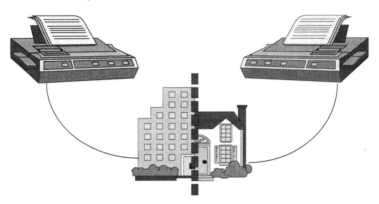

Figure 4.3. To fax or not to fax? To be formal or not be formal?

Basically, there are two kinds of FAX—they are *formal* and *informal*. The cover sheet gives a clue to which kind you are using. A *formal fax* is sent to someone you do not know well or who works in a large company where fax machines are shared among many people. In this case, you will always want to include a cover sheet. You will also want to include enough information so that the fax can get to its intended party.

An *informal fax* is one that goes to a small office or perhaps even a home office. It rarely needs a cover sheet. You will follow the guidelines for informal faxes to someone you know well and who has a private fax machine at his or her disposal.

Formal Faxes

A *formal fax* should always use a fax cover sheet (see Figure 4.4). Make sure you include the following information directly on the cover sheet: addressee's name, title, department, phone, location, number of pages transmitted, time and date of transmission; request for confirmation of receipt; sender information; name, address, voice telephone number, fax number; and any special instructions for sending a return message.

Your Company's Name Here

FACSIMILE COVER SHEET

To:	Mr. John Doe
Company:	ABC Company
Phone:	(Area Code) Their Voice Phone-Number
Fax:	(Area Code) Their Fax-Number
From:	Ms. Cheryl Currid
Company:	Currid & Company
Phone:	(Area Code) Your Voice Phone-Number
Fax:	(Area Code) Your Fax-Number
Date:	Today
Pages including this cover page:	(the actual number of pages sent)

Comments: Here are my comments in response to your letter and proposal.

Figure 4.4. Example of a formal fax cover sheet that shows the required information.

There are times when you will want the return message to come by telephone or e-mail instead of fax. This is especially helpful when privacy is a consideration.

Remember that faxes, even with a cover sheet, are not secure. They are available for many eyes to view. Unless you are sure that your intended party is standing at the other end of the fax line, do not send highly confidential information by fax.

Informal Faxes

For *informal faxes*, you do not need a separate cover page, but you should at least put the name of the person to whom you are sending the fax, your name, your telephone and fax numbers, as well as how many pages you are sending on the first sheet you send. With this information, your associate, client, or friend will know how many pages to expect and will not have to search for the numbers when making a reply.

Tips for Sending Faxes

While there is no official standard for fax etiquette, there are some common sense rules you should follow. They include:

- **Use page headers.** Most fax equipment will let you program a header line that appears on the top of each page you send. Always include your company name, fax number, and page count as a header on each faxed page.
- **Tell receiver how many pages you are sending.** Whether you use a formal cover sheet or not, you should mark somewhere on the first page of your fax how many pages will follow. That way, if there is a problem and the fax gets cut off, the person receiving the fax will know he or she did not get the full package.
- **Use attractive fax cover sheets.** Many people have gotten creative with their fax cover sheets. If you are sending to people who receive lots of faxes, a designer

fax or catchy phrase on the fax cover sheet will help separate it from others.

- **Keep your faxes short.** Nobody enjoys getting a 23-page fax, and you will not enjoy sending it when you get the long distance telephone bill either. Use care and consideration for sending faxes that are way too long.

- **Watch print size and fonts.** If you are using a standard fax machine, be careful about the size, font, and quality of the document you are using. If possible, do not use very small fonts or pages that have been reduced by a copy machine. The document will not be very readable on the other end. Also, Helvetica style fonts fax more clearly than others. These include fonts like the True Type font Arial, Univers, and non-Serif (or fonts without little feet).

Receiving Faxes

Receiving faxes is still tricky in some organizations. Since most organizations do not want to equip every person with his or her own fax device and phone line, faxes need to be shared. And, sharing immediately brings questions about security. Depending on your individual office situation, you may need to have a set of procedures that deal with the distribution of the hard copy, security, and contacting the sender when there is a problem with the received fax.

Look! His secretary is coming to get his fax. We better hurry and read this.

Figure 4.5. Sharing a fax machine immediately brings up the question of security when sending sensitive information.

Some large companies assign the job of distributing faxes to a receptionist or staff secretary. In some cases, the faxes may be put into interoffice envelopes and distributed with the company's internal mail. This type of distribution is a throwback to the bad (and slow) old days and defeats the purpose of faxing—to get documents from here to there quickly.

If you make use of fax technology combined with LAN technology, you may also want to investigate the use of automatic, inbound routing techniques. It is possible to set up your receiving fax unit to scan for the addressee and automatically route it into his or her electronic mail box. This technology is still new and not widely supported.

BEWARE OF JUNK FAX

No sooner does a technology get popular, than somebody figures out a way to exploit it. Enter the junk fax vendors.

Already in many cities, firms have sprung up to flood your fax machine with unsolicited and sometimes unwanted information and advertisements. Even if you do not publish your fax number, clever vendors have found ways of locating it. Some of them have used computer devices that autodial a block of phone numbers, then record the ones where a fax tone was detected.

Figure 4.6. Junk faxes can overwhelm you.

Some fax advertising firms have tried to make junk fax a little more respectable. For example, a firm called ADVERFAX sends you advertisements that look like white page copies from the telephone company's yellow pages. Periodically, ADVERFAX will send its customers a roll of fax paper to make up for what it used (a nice touch).

Tips For Receiving Faxes

There are always simpler ways of doing things, and these are the five tips I recommend for receiving faxes more efficiently in todays business:

- **Promote fax efficiency.** Fax perpetuates people's dependence on paper. There is no easy way out of it. Study your office's faxing habits and make sure you are not faxing or receiving faxes when an e-mail or voice mail would do. If your office or workgroup receives a lot of faxes, consider buying a plain paper fax, a printer fax, or a PC fax board on your network. (See the discussion of technology options later in this chapter.)
- **Copy important documents at once.** If you use a thermal-paper based fax machine, make a habit of copying the fax on a copy machine right away. Fax paper and the print on it will fade over time. Better yet, junk that old fax machine and get a plain paper unit. It will save you plenty of time, aggravation, and money over time.
- **Keep a supply of fax paper.** If you use a thermal-paper based fax machine, you are a prisoner of your fax paper supply. Always keep an extra roll or two around. Remember, should you run out, you could be out of business. Most fax machines have limited abilities to store up documents in memory—so you are out of luck if there is no fax paper in the office. Losing an important document (or never knowing about it) could present an embarrassing business situation.

- **Find a place for confidential faxes.** If someone is going to get a confidential fax, make sure there is a place for it to be properly handled. In some organizations, you may have to set up multiple fax lines just to deal with the security issue. Some companies place a "secure" fax station at the desk of the departmental secretary. He or she becomes the custodian of confidential faxes and makes sure all incoming faxes are properly protected and routed only to the appropriate person(s).

- **Discourage "junk fax."** Getting a lot of junk fax is not only a waste of paper, it is a waste of time. If you find your office is getting a lot of unwanted faxes, call the junk fax sender and ask to be taken off the list. Since junk faxing is a relatively new business, you will probably find the senders willing to work with you. If they do not and the problem persists, have the fax number changed and alert everyone who needs the correct number. Keep in mind that changing numbers (even to unlisted or nonpublished numbers) is only a temporary measure. Junk fax kings with autodialers will eventually find you again.

FAX OPTIONS: TECHNOLOGY

Despite its humble beginnings and very long gestation period, fax technology has made quantum leaps in the last ten years. There are three basic flavors of fax equipment on the market today: stand-alone fax machines, PC fax or fax/modem units for personal computers (and their network cousins, fax servers), and, as discussed in

Figure 4.7. Message-sending has come a long way over the past several years.

the last chapter, multi-function products (MFU) that rely on fax as their primary selling feature. Each flavor of fax technology has its own special benefits and is right for different uses.

So What's the Right Fax Technology?

It turns out, the right office solution for many places might be multiple technologies used by different people for different applications. Since fax is such a low-cost technology, it is not unreasonable to think that you might end up with more than one way to send a fax.

Stand-alone Fax Machines

By far, the most popular form of fax equipment is the stand-alone fax machine. Dedicated fax machines are inexpensive, readily available at most office supply stores, and easy to plug in and set up. Costing between $300 and $600 (depending on features) these machines are within the financial reach of small and large companies alike—even personal users with home offices find it an inexpensive convenience.

While there is no set standard for installing a fax machine, most companies install them within workgroups or in common areas of an office building floor. The copy machine room often turns out to be the fax receiving room.

Besides a wide array of calling or receiving features, stand-alone fax machines are distinguished by the type of paper they use. Most inexpensive fax machines use a specially coated paper that is sold in

Figure 4.8. There are no set standards for placement of fax machines, but installing them within workgroups is a practical solution.

rolls. While the paper is handy, many people find it difficult to work with. It tends to curl up, and sometimes is difficult to feed through a copier. Also, as mentioned earlier in the chapter, the print on fax paper is likely to fade over time. If the faxed document is important, it should be copied onto regular paper.

Plain paper fax machines, while more expensive, are a more appropriate choice for a busy office that receives a lot of faxes. They use plain, low-cost copy paper and save the step of having to copy every incoming fax.

PC Fax or Fax/Modem Units

Just as the fax machine threatens to make local mail and bicycle messengers extinct, the PC fax or fax/modem units may make standard stand-alone fax machines obsolete. If you use your PC to create most of your documents such as memos, letters, and forms that you fax, you might consider investing in a PC fax or fax/modem. These come as adapter cards that will fit into a standard internal expansion slot of a PC, or as a small external device.

And, for road warriors, there is good news. Most portable computer modems are actually fax/modems. If you set up the software correctly, you will be able to send a fax to someone about as easily as you can print it. In fact, the fax/modem actually configures itself as a printer option. But, instead of printing, you send your document over the phone lines to somebody's fax.

Features and Benefits of PC Fax

Faxes can be sent faster and more efficiently if they are sent directly from your computer rather than a stand-alone fax machine. Depending on the hardware/software you use, it can be a one-step process. Computer-generated faxes can also be stored for sending at a later time. For example, you may wish to batch up a number of outgoing faxes and send them all at lunch time while you are away from your desk, or send them in the middle of the night when telephone long distance rates are lower.

With a PC fax you can also send broadcast faxes, that is, faxes sent to groups of people. Sending out faxes this way can be much more efficient than standing over a hot fax machine for hours, inputting 40 or 50 telephone numbers and putting the documents back in the fax machine by hand.

Faxes sent from your computer or LAN server can be sent with high resolution, called FINE mode, while stand-alone faxes normally use a less-definitive STANDARD mode. That means, if both you and the recipient of your fax have capable equipment, your documents will come out much clearer with fewer jagged edges.

Figure 4.9. From your PC fax, you can send faxes to groups without having to stand and dial the numbers by hand.

Price tags for fax/modems, which run at high data-transmission speeds, run about $60–300. The more expensive units incorporate the same fax capabilities as the less-expensive ones, but offer very high speed modems (from 9600 to 28.8 bits per second) and compression capabilities.

PC Fax Drawbacks

For the most part, PC fax technology makes sending faxes easier, but not receiving them. They can be hooked up to a stand-alone PC or installed on a LAN for shared use. When the right hardware/software is installed, sending faxes is as easy as printing a document. Receiving them either on a LAN or stand-alone PC, however, requires a little extra work because the technology for automated routing of incoming faxes is still not well implemented.

Some fax/modem cards, like the Complete Communicator, can also perform other functions like managing your voice mail. The modem digitizes phone messages and stores them on your hard drive.

WORDS ARE NOT WORDS ON A FAX

Keep in mind that even if you are sending or receiving text through a PC fax unit, the device does not see the words as words, it sees them as a graphic. Faxes either sent or received with a fax board (or external fax unit for Macs) are converted to PC graphics files (either proprietary formats or standard formats like, PCX, TIFF, etc.). They are stored on the PC as a graphic image.

Viewing or printing faxes from a PC requires the use of special fax (or graphic) viewing software. You should also know that fax files can be a bit like Miss Piggy when it comes to disk space. Sometimes they can occupy as much as a megabyte/page. Faxes received by a PC fax can also take a long time to print, as much as one minute for each page on a standard laser printer.

With the limitations of graphics file conversion, many vendors incorporate OCR (optical character recognition) technology in their fax software. This software converts incoming faxes into text files or even documents specific to your word-processing software, and they require very little disk space. So you can edit, store, or print the text. These faxes do not look exactly like the original documents and they lose an element of security. For example, someone could edit the text version of an incoming fax before it reaches the designated recipient.

GROWTH OF PC FAX TECHNOLOGY

Although fax technology has become a must for business today, the real growth is coming from intelligent fax products. These include specialized software and hardware that allow people to build fax services.

Fax-on-Demand

Fax services such as fax-on-demand make it easy for a customer to retrieve information such as marketing brochures, product literature, and catalog information. If you are a customer, you will find most systems easy and convenient to use. If you are a business person looking for a low-cost way to improve your own company's services, look here.

Here is how the standard system works. Let's say you want to get some product literature from ABC Tool Company. You pick up the phone and call the company you want to receive information from on one or more products or services. A voice mail-type system answers your call and prompts you to key in numbers on your touch-tone phone to order the information. You then enter your fax number and the system automatically faxes you the product information.

For example, technology maker Intel has an excellent service called FaxBack. A customer simply has to call the service and request documents or literature by a document number. If you do not know the document number, you can request a fax that lists all available documents. The dialog goes something like this:

Thank you for calling Intel, makers of the Pentium Processor. This is FaxBack. The menus have changed so please listen carefully.

Press 1 for the Main Menu or 2 for FaxBack Help.

Before we can send you anything, we will need to know what kind of machine we will be sending to. If you have a fax machine, please press 0. Or if you have an Intel FaxCard, press 1.

This is FaxBack's Main Menu. If you know the document number you need, you may place an express order by pressing the 1 key now. If you would like Fax-Back's Table of Contents faxed to you, press 2.

Companies use fax-on-demand to supply pages from their catalogs, price sheets, technical support, subscription forms, and even newsletters.

Other Fax Services

Some public libraries are beginning to offer fax-back services so researchers can request fax copies of articles instead of driving to the library. It is expensive—$10 an article—but you save time and expense by not driving 25–50 miles and paying for parking. Another library is using fax to advertise their monthly book sales.

Restaurants are learning how to let customers fax forward. They let customers fax in their orders or confirm reservations. Even some McDonald's let you fax an order. They will have it ready for you when you drive through.

Building Your Own Fax on Demand Service

FastFacts developed by The Programmer's Shop in Hingham, Massachusetts, developed the first 24-hour, fully automated "Instant Action Literature Request Service." The system stores a detailed catalog and provides an index with a brief product description and code for you to use when you call for the detailed information.

Today you can get fax-on-demand software as a stand-alone product or as a feature integrated into a voice-mail system. Either way, these systems require a dedicated PC—special software to handle the voice and fax—and a voice board as well as a fax board. Since many new computers come equipped with the modem and voice capability, chances are you will not have to do much upgrading of your hardware.

SOME FAX DOS AND DON'TS

Okay, so fax technology offers lots of communication options. But, let's get back to basics for a few minutes. Here is a list of DOs and DON'Ts for fax users:

- **DO use a fax cover sheet with faxes you send to other companies.** Unless you know you are sending the fax to someone's desk, use a formal approach to faxing. The cover sheet makes it easier for the recipient to locate his or her fax, particularly if your company's logo stands out in bold.
- **DO confirm your fax transmittals.** Fax is stable and reliable technology, but not bulletproof. If you do not hear from your addressee in a couple of days, it is a good idea to follow up with a phone call.
- **If you are sending graphics, DO check with your recipient to determine if he or she has fine resolution on their fax machine.** If not, you may want to transmit the graphics file directly to one of their PCs via high-speed modems.
- **DO use a fax modem when most of your outgoing faxed documents are computer-generated.** If you send many memos, letters, and forms, most fax modems now have easy-to-use software that makes faxing a document from your workstation almost as easy as printing it. You will save lots of time and money—no printing of documents to fax them, less fax paper for incoming documents, and no requirement for an attendant at the fax machine.
- **DO send long distance faxes at night when the telephone rates are lower.** Few people think about the

cost of faxing until somebody has to pay the telephone bill. Fax bills can and do add up. If your fax does not absolutely, positively have to go now, hold it up in a queue and have it sent at night. This could save more money than you think.

- **DON'T use the company fax machine for your personal fax without checking with the boss.** Use a little common sense and business ethics. You do not want your resume to wind up in his hands. If you send it long distance, someone will be reviewing the telephone bill and want to know who sent a fax to The Alaskan Oil Company or ARAMCO in Saudi Arabia. Those faxes cost at least $5 each.

- **DON'T encourage your correspondents to send personal mail via fax to your office.** The fax machine attendant, his or her friends, boss, and others may want to read some juicy personal correspondence. Office rumors are easy enough to start, do not fuel them with facts from a fax.

- **DON'T buy a stand-alone fax machine or a fax modem without considering how they will be used.** Remember, a fax machine requires an attendant—at least part time—to change the paper and distribute the faxes. A fax modem card in a PC can receive faxes 24 hours a day just like a fax machine, but you may have to dedicate the machine to fax traffic if it is used by busy people, such as in the sales department. Sending faxes by modem can become a highly efficient process. For example, with automatic dialing, you can set up your system to send a fax late at night when the rates are lowest, or to broadcast the same message to a list of people after you have gone home.

- **DON'T install a fax modem in a LAN server without considering who will distribute the faxes to the individual workstations.** Assigning an extra job to your LAN administrator, who may already have too many tasks supporting and training users, may be the last straw. You might, however, designate the task to an assistant LAN administrator or a want-to-be-administrator. If you arrange to have incoming faxes routed to a printer for users to pick up at their convenience, you should purchase a fax machine—that is what it is for.

- **DON'T encourage junk faxes.** If you start receiving lots of junk fax, immediately call the sender and ask to be taken off the list. If that does not work, and you do not wish to change the fax phone number, then threaten to call the Federal Communications Commission or your attorney, who will file a legal suit for violation of your privacy. With a fax modem, some of the software allows you to scan your incoming faxes before you print; delete any junk faxes from the batch. Often you only need to read a line or two before you know if it is junk.

- **DO use OCR.** A good optical character recognition (OCR) program that will read a PC file and convert the fax graphic to ASCII is important if you purchase a fax modem. The technology is not 100-percent perfect, but it is good enough for most text applications. You might not want to OCR a fax of your checking account statement, fearing misread numbers, but it is fine for most letters.

- **DO consider a fax modem or PC modem-to-modem communications for sending or receiving a long report.** Long reports should be transmitted at night, whether sent by fax or modem, to avoid tying up the fax or PC with the fax modem card and to save money on your telephone bill.

- **DO remember that the fax modem may not replace the fax machine.** But, it can serve as a supplement. It is the right tool for sending faxes that already exist on disk and for receiving faxes privately at your convenience. You can print them on real paper without using the copy machine.

- **DO consider a fax modem that has the ability to detect and negotiate a common transmission rate.** It not only matches transmission rates with the receiving modems, but it can give you the highest rate of data transfer, compression, and error control as soon as it identifies the same features in the other modem. Choose a fax modem with an automatic fallback feature that will prevent re-sending large blocks of data by changing transmission to a slower but more reliable speed. Advanced modems can fall forward once they sense that line conditions are favorable, but this feature is found more commonly in 9,600-bps or higher speed boards.

  Fax modems with auto-dialing and auto-answering let you automate communications without you sitting at your computer. Auto-dialing lets the modem work on its own so you can set up a fax transmission for night time. If you have an auto-answering feature, this lets you call the receiving fax modem and send a fax from a remote site. So, you could send a message through to your computer while on the road or pull a file down to your remote location. Finally, you will appreciate the ability to hear what your modem is doing. When you hear the fax modem dialing and the screech of the connecting PC or fax machine, it lets you know that you have gotten through. You may have to adjust the volume using a knob on an external modem or use built-in software control.

- **DO use faxes for permanent records and audit trail documents.** Why? Faxes are very effective permanent records and can be used to substitute for voice mail. When you want to be very specific—using catalog numbers, product descriptions, price quotations, etc.— a fax can eliminate misunderstanding or a listener's transposing numbers when using the telephone.

HOW TO USE A STANDARD FAX MACHINE

If you are clueless about how to use a fax machine, and have never used a fax machine on your own, read this section. This takes you through some of the basics and describes some standard fax options and frequently used keys. Better yet, read this section, then a copy of the fax user's guide that came with the machine at your office.

Standard Fax Options

Today, standard fax machines in your office or home may have a variety of features. Here are some of the basic operations you can perform:

Dial—Dials telephone or fax numbers without lifting the handset.

Hold—Can place incoming calls on hold. You need this when your fax runs out of paper.

Redial/Pause—Tries the last number dialed again when an outgoing call failed to connect for any reason. It inserts a pause when you are dialing through a PBX (the combination telephone switch and computer installed in your building) to allow time for the connection.

One-Touch Dial and Speed-Dial Key—Allows you to press a function key or enter a code for a fax number stored in the Fax's memory.

Numeric Keyboard—Works just like a touch-tone telephone.

Liquid Crystal Display Screen—A 16–20 character, alphanumeric liquid crystal display (LCD), which displays helpful messages, phone numbers, and the current date and time. When you slip a document to be faxed into the machine, it displays: "Enter Fax Number."

THE FUTURE OF FAX

There is no doubt that fax technology is going to change. I believe that, ultimately, fax will disappear and be replaced by enhanced (but easier to use) e-mail systems.

Fax has many redeeming qualities. It is quick, low-cost, and a wonderfully simple technology. It can quickly get information around to people who can annotate it (mark it up) and send it back.

Fax is easy to maintain. It does not need special software, batteries to be charged, or other attentions. It just works.

But, we will not stop here. There is more to technology than perpetuating paper—and fax is guilty of doing just that.

So how else can we communicate thoughts and ideas in business? Stay tuned. The next chapter covers another technology that has been infiltrating our offices: voice mail.

5

Victory Over Voice

Voice technology used to be easy. In fact, many of us let it invade our homes long before it infiltrated our offices. Remember the little innocent telephone answering machine? For less than a $100 and about five minutes worth of installation time, anybody could set up a reliable little gizmo to answer the phone, take messages, and play them back later.

It was so easy, just record a simple message. You could create something clever, serious, or something in-between. The message could be long or short, like:

> *Hi, this is Bob. I'm not here. At the sound*
> *of the beep, leave me a message and I will*
> *call you back.*

Installation was simple. All Bob had to do was plug in the answering machine, record that simple message, flip a switch and it was done. The little machine dutifully answered the calls when Bob was not there, took the messages, and played them back when he wanted them.

So much for the good old days. Today, most businesses have found their way to technology-assisted voice processing, called voice messaging (or voice mail).

We have hired "Silicon Sally" or "Silicon Sam" to answer our phones. We have given everyone in the office a voice mail box; and we installed megabytes (costing megabucks) worth of gear to record incoming and outgoing chatter. Voice messaging options have taken a skyward leap when it comes to functionality, complexity, and cost.

Figure 5.1. Silicon Sam may be answering the phone when you call.

This chapter is dedicated to voice processing. It might get you thinking that you are hearing things, maybe even virtual voices. It takes both a philosophical plus a pragmatic look at voice technology, where voice processing fits in the office, how it can help, and when it does not work well at all. Voice messaging systems are changing, and as the technology changes, each iteration provides you with more options. The system that you thought was cold and distant yesterday, could turn out to be warm and friendly today. You be the judge.

During this chapter, I will discuss some tips on setting up your own office voice mail boxes and give you a few tricks and traps. I honestly believe that voice mail can be a productive component to the 21st century business person. It only takes a few minor changes in your habits before you turn into a real voice processing pro.

Finally, I will close this chapter with some case examples showing what some companies considered when they looked for and brought in the voice invaders.

IN THE BEGINNING. . .

Electronic voice processing or "voice mail" first became popular in the early 1980s. The technology had existed long before, but it was not cheap enough (err. . . economically feasible) until microprocessor and memory technology became pocket change for most organizations.

Like the other electronic technology, such as fax and e-mail, it created more social havoc than technical trauma. From the very beginning, voice messaging systems were relatively stable and riskless. But, then again, getting the technology installed is always the easy part.

Accepting voice messaging as a viable business tool was not quite so easy. At first, nobody liked it. Frequently, it was not welcomed by either company workers or callers. Secretaries and receptionists hated it because they felt they lost control over the phones (and some choice office gossip). In fact, some companies saw this technology as a way to rid themselves of receptionists and a few other administrative and clerical positions.

Many would-be callers did not like office voice mail either. People would often complain "Hey, I do not want to talk to a machine. I want to talk to a real person." Although machines take more accurate messages and were available all the time, callers griped about how impersonal voice mail made companies.

Figure 5.2. Initially, voice mail was not a welcome addition to every office setting.

There was (and remains) a suspicion that some people hide behind voice mail. They use voice mail to selectively screen calls and avoid difficult situations.

But, despite the rocky start, voice messaging had too much going for it to be snuffed out. It has grown to be over a billion dollars a year business and revenues have doubled since 1988.

Figure 5.3. Some people hide behind voice mail to avoid confrontations.

It does help free up staff to handle other tasks and gives back a loyal, dedicated worker that stays on duty 24 hours a day, 7 days a week, 365 days a year without ever complaining or asking for raises. Moreover, it opens the door for solving other administrative and communication needs, such as setting up a number to call when someone wants to hear the latest company stock price, notice of snow days, or other special company announcements.

GOOD AND BAD NEWS ABOUT VOICE MAIL

Along with technology, voice messaging brings in many cultural changes. If used correctly, it can become an efficient tool for the office. Misused, however, it can turn into an invisible wall for people to hide behind or, if overused, a time consuming bore. It can also generate less-than-efficient processes if people use it for the wrong applications.

Good Uses

Among the good news that voice messaging brings to office environments are:

- **Terminates telephone tag:** Voice messaging's greatest accomplishment is that it lets people put an end to

Figure 5.4. You are it! Telephone tag can be eliminated when you have the capability of leaving a voice message.

telephone tag. This single feature is worth a lot.

According to several studies, two-thirds to three-quarters of all business calls are not completed on the first attempt. These statistics have tremendous costs associated with them. Not only does the meter keep running on multiple missed phone calls (often long distance toll calls) but it also wastes people's time. Since time is a very precious and expensive resource, time lost cannot be easily calculated or recaptured—but, everyone knows it robs companies. You just do not know how much, and you probably never will.

According to one study, however, a company can cut the cost of calls by as much as 40 percent by just installing voice mail. I believe that savings count for a lot of the difficulties.

- **Lets you communicate at different times, from different places:** Another benefit is that voice mail does

Figure 5.5. Voice mail lets you communicate across time zones.

not require both people at the same time. A caller can leave a message at one time, the receiver can respond at another time, and the follow-up can take place later. This is a great advantage for time zone separated colleagues. No more waiting until 3:00 A.M. local time to hear from your fellow workers on the other side of the planet.

- **Conveys emotion:** A sometimes forgotten benefit of voice messaging is that it can convey emotion. In our fast, furious, fax and e-mail world, we can sometimes forget how much a kind and gentle word can mean. Voice, unlike other forms of "different time, different place" communications, can transmit emotion along with the words. It can be used very effectively to make a point.

- **Compresses call time:** In most cases, voice mail messages are shorter than real-time calls. Since few people engage in chit-chat with machines, they are less likely to talk about the football scores, company politics, or the details of George's great presentation. Instead, recorded voice messages tend to be shorter and more to the point. This saves both time and money.

Bad Uses

But, all is not paradise with voice mail enabled corporate culture. When under- or over-used, they can wreak havoc with standard office procedures. Consider the following:

- **Death on details:** Voice messages have many benefits, but recording many details is not among them. While it

Figure 5.6. For all its virtues, voice messaging is not perfect for everything.

might be fine to leave a message about the great job that Harry did over at the customer's shop, you probably do not want to send him a 17-point follow up report. If you do, you will waste both Harry's and your time just trying to write down all 17 points. Besides, if Harry is not a graduate speed writer, he will probably have to start, stop, and rewind the message several times before he gets them all down.

- **Cannot sort them:** Voice messages are recorded, and played back on a first-come-first-served basis. There is no way to sort them. You cannot re-order the 15 messages in your voice mail box by most important caller to least important.
- **Cannot skim them:** While some voice messaging systems let you stop playing a message and move on to the next one, few let you fast forward so you can only listen to certain parts. Count on having a couple of cups of coffee during voice mail retrieval sessions if your colleagues have the habit of leaving six-minute messages (if your system allows them).

- **Harder to manage than e-mail:** Voice messages can be saved on most systems, but not as easily as e-mail. Voice messages take up a lot of disk space, and therefore most systems are limited to the number of messages a person can realistically save. Moreover, few voice systems let you save messages in an organized method, such as in subject folders. So, if over time you collect 50 saved voice messages, you could have to go through 49 before you find the one that Aunt Martha sent three weeks ago.
- **Multiple voice mail systems do not talk to each other:** Although some voice messaging systems can forward messages or page you and let you know a message has come in, most systems are not smart enough to interoperate with each other. Pity the poor electronically empowered person who has a voice messaging system at the office, an answering machine at home, and voice mail connected with his or her cellular phone. Chances are none of these systems work together and the person takes more time than is saved to check each system for messages.
- **Overuse, misuse, abuse can waste time:** Like many things, voice messaging has benefits when used in the right ways, but it can be productivity poison if misused. Often, the biggest problem people have with voice messaging is starting to become overly dependent and using the systems for more than short, non-detailed messages.

Figure 5.7. Overuse and abuse of voice mail can waste time.

The manager who insists on sending out four and five minute messages, four times a week to all 20 of his subordinates is probably not too popular. Especially if he or she records them in the middle of the night so the staff has to wade through them in the rush of starting up the next day.

Moreover, voice mail does not make a good order-entry system, claims-payment system, inventory-record system, or anything else that is likely to create many detailed records. Fax, e-mail, or other forms of electronic data transfer are much better alternatives.

MULTIPLE CHOICES: VOICE MAIL OPTIONS

Voice messaging systems come in many shapes, sizes, and flavors. The feature list, along with prices, can vary widely. Most office-oriented systems cover the basics of letting people record greetings, store messages, retrieve messages—then add lots of gravy features.

Options that extend the basics of message taking include:

- **Computer Telephone Integration (CTI):** The big news for voice technology is the merger between voice and computers. Today most new voice processing systems are actually computer systems with a voice board. All the features are built into software. There are hundreds of options with these systems, such as fax on demand, order entry, databases access to report on balances, and other features.

  Companies like Salt Lake City-based CallWare push the state of the art with a Windows graphical interface and advanced features. CallWare runs on a Novell local area network and offers advanced features for call management.

- **Interactive Voice Response (IVR):** This is a handy technology that comes with some high-end, voice-processing systems. It lets people interact directly with data using your phone system. The objective: Try to simplify your life and the lives of your customers, business partners, and colleagues.

The technology lets people dial in and directly interact with computers and computer-stored data by using the push buttons on their telephones. For example, many banks have installed IVR technology so that customers can call up and get deposit information, hear their checking account balances, or get the latest rates on savings certificates. The computer systems are generally very easy for the customer to operate and, unlike human information systems, they do not risk giving out the wrong information because a teller misreads a number.

- **Automated attendants:** An automated attendant is like a voice robot. Its sole purpose in life is to move calls to the right person (or person's mailbox). The attendant is a computer program that answers the phone, plays a prerecorded greeting to callers and helps them route their call. The program might let the caller branch out to hear a listing of a company directory, look up specific names by spelling out someone's name, locate the proper department, or other tasks.

  Some companies have already moved the entire phone-answering process from a human being to a computer. If you are considering this, make sure you use a robust voice messaging system capable of online administration, performing a directory search (to look up the extension number of an employee), and individual mailbox customization. It is also helpful to tightly integrate voice mail with the individual phone sets in the office so that people can see a message waiting light.

- **Call accounting systems:** Call accounting is a "big brother" logging system that lets you see who made what calls. They produce reports that show the details of all calls made by a person's telephone extension.

  Companies use them to monitor call activity and hopefully discourage people from making too many personal calls or unnecessary long distance calls. In the spirit of the old saying "you cannot manage what you cannot measure," these systems are the measurement tools. Industry experts estimate call accounting can save companies from 5 to 25 percent on phone bills if people manage what they measure.

- **Voice loggers:** Sometimes call accounting systems are not enough. Certain business situations require an even "bigger brother" to monitor business. Simply having a record of who called what number is not enough. A detailed record of the conversation is required. This requires voice-logging technology, which actually makes a recording of the voice conversations.

  Stock brokers are frequently customers of voice logging systems. They use them to record transactions when customers want to buy or sell stocks. That way, if there is a question whether the customer said "buy more" or "sell all" of a certain stock, the voice recording can serve as a record.

- **People paging:** Voice systems offer several types of paging options, both internal and external. Internal paging allows the caller to actually issue a page for someone in case he or she does not answer the phone. External paging is set up to automatically call a pager and let someone know there is mail in his or her voice mail box.

  Paging, either internal or external, can save both time and money. By attempting to locate the person, it is likely a conversation can be completed in the first try or a callback can take place right away. (See Chapter 6 for more information about paging.)

- **Security for Direct Inward System Access (DISA):** A final feature found in many voice systems is a feature that allows callers to call in, then get an outside line to dial out. This feature can be a phone hacker's haven and cost your company thousands of dollars.

  While it is helpful for legitimate employees who are on the road, and want to make long distance calls using the company's low-cost lines, it can also give phone hackers free access to long distance services.

Add-on security devices can be used to stop hackers. These devices make it necessary for the caller to use a special password to get an outside line.

THE BASICS: VOICE MAIL FOR HUMAN BEINGS

There are a few basic requirements to get started on most voice messaging systems. Consult your owner's guide for the specifics of what keys you should push to set up your own system.

At first, you should make sure your voice mail box is set up to do a few basic chores. It should play a recorded greeting, take messages, and play back messages. You can move on to more exotic functions later.

Generally speaking, the process of setting up a voice mail box makes you only perform a few simple tasks. Chances are that someone has already hooked up your telephone and extension into the system, and all you will have to do is answer some prompts, select a password, record your name and a message.

Setting Up Voice Mail

Your voice mail box is like your voice valet. It is there to help you when you need it. It will greet your callers with a recorded message when you are busy or cannot or do not choose to answer the phone. It will take messages for you; it will play back messages when you want to hear them.

You should follow a few commonsense tips to keep things simple and friendly when you first set up your voice mail box.

Great Greetings

Your voice mail greeting is a "virtual you" when you are not around. It should reflect you and your business personality as much as possible and be within the bounds of good taste.

Ideally, your recorded voice mail greeting should be warm and friendly. It should invite the caller to leave you a message and talk to you. You will want to make callers comfortable about leaving you a personal message and not just their names and phone numbers.

Here are a few ideas for setting up your greeting:

- **Never delegate your greeting.** It does not matter how big a job you have or how important you are, voice

Figure 5.8. Voice mail greetings are your opportunity to personally touch your caller. Try to use a pleasant, cheery voice for your message.

mail greetings are your opportunity to personally touch your caller. They should reflect you, and the very best of you. Never, never, never let someone else record your voice greeting. It is condescending, snobbish, boorish, and rude.

- **Use the shortest possible greeting.** Do not bore your callers with every last detail of your name, job title, life history, kid's basketball score, and current whereabouts. Make your greeting simple and to the point.

Using your most professional but cheery voice, choose words that invite your caller to leave a message for you. Be sure your greeting identifies you, that you cannot answer the phone, and encourages them to leave a detailed message. Generally speaking, the friendlier the greeting, the more likely you will get people to leave you a message.

- **Give callers an escape hatch.** If your voice messaging system lets callers bypass your greeting or ring someone else's extension, let your caller know it. This information is best given early in the message, especially if you have a message over 25 or 30 seconds.
- **Use humor sparingly.** Everybody likes a good joke, but your voice mail greeting might not be the place to tell them. Slapstick or humorous greetings do not have a home in most business environments. Unless your corporate culture is extremely casual, or you are in the joke-writing business, do not begin your voice mail greeting with, *"Say, did you hear about the one where. . ."*
- **Use date or event specific greetings.** If you have a system that makes it easy to maintain multiple greetings, and you maintain them, feel free to use greetings that give your callers a little information about your activity. Messages that include passages like:

  > *I will be in meetings until 2:00 today. . . or*
  >
  > *I am out of town on vacation until Tuesday the 25th, or*
  >
  > *Joe Smith, extension 122, is handling my projects. . .*

  are helpful to your callers.
- **Tell your callers about edit options.** Depending on what features your voice mail system offers, you may wish to tell your callers they can edit their messages. For example, you may include in your greeting:

You can press the star key on your tele-
phone to review your message after you
have recorded it.

This lets the caller know he or she has some options if a mistake is made. Most voice mail systems
will handle the details of what prompts your callers
need to use when they edit a message.

Sample Personal Greetings

The following greetings are offered as suggestions and
food for thought. Use them as outlines and customize
them for your own specific situation.

Each of them sets up a friendly and informative
note. They all encourage the caller to take action.

Hi. This is Jane Doe. I am away from my desk
right now, but I will return your call as soon as I
get back. Please leave your name, message and
telephone number. You can press the star key on
your telephone if you need to review your message,
or hang up when you are finished.

Jane's message is standard voice mail fare. It is
simple, direct, and to the point. Notice that Jane asks her
callers to leave their information in the order of: name,
message, and phone number. She does this for a purpose.
Since her mail system lets her listen to messages, then
play back the entire message, or just the last eight seconds of the message, she is trying to encourage the caller
into leaving the phone number last. That way, if Jane
needs to listen to the phone number again, she does not
have to wade through the entire message again.

Hello. This is Jim Smith and it is Monday, De-
cember 14. I will be in meetings until 2:00 today,
but if you will leave me your name, message, and
phone number, I will return your call. If you
would rather talk to my assistant, Julie, please
press the pound key, then dial 123.

Jim's message accomplishes two goals: personal touch and setting up expectations. It is also time-sensitive. He offers a personal touch by expressing the current day and date. That tells the caller he is there. He then sets up his callers' expectations by telling them he will not be able to start returning calls until after 2:00. He offers an alternative in case his callers need to talk to someone right away. One note of caution for messages like Jim's, make sure you have another message for the next day. It is bad business form to have an incorrect message with day and date. Do not let that message slip to Tuesday.

> *This is George Clark. I am on vacation this week but Susan Blaze is taking care of my projects. You can reach Susan by pressing the pound key, then dialing 4023. Otherwise, feel free to leave me a message that I will return when I get back next week.*

George's message again sets the callers' expectations and offers an alternative to waiting for him. He has told callers that he is not around, that he is on vacation, and that somebody else can help them. This message invites the caller to take the appropriate action depending on how important the message is.

> *Hi. This is Bill Jones. I am on special assignment right now and cannot take your call. You can interrupt this greeting and begin recording a message immediately by pressing 9 or transfer to another person by pressing pound and the person's extension number. If you are calling about the Lake Charles project, please call Ann Smith at extension 1243; the Denver project, contact George Greer at 5023; the Boston project, contact Bill Buyers at 2034; or the Los Angeles project, contact Larry Lutz, at 3496. For all other inquires, press the pound key and dial 0 for a company operator.*

Bill's message is a long one, but gives callers an escape hatch right away. In this case, he has offered callers several alternatives for transferring or getting help. Notice also that he has reduced the number of words he uses as he goes down the list of call alternatives. Once the tone and main message were conveyed, he used as few words as possible to give out the details.

Techniques for Recording Your Greeting

Your greeting may only last a few seconds, but it will be played over and over to everyone who calls when you are not there. At the risk of sounding like a stage mother, you should put your best voice forward. Here are a few tips for making that recording a good one.

- **Write it down first:** Even if your voice mail greeting is a short one, it will be easier to record it if it is written down. Write down or type up your greeting so that you can read it in case you forget a word or two.
- **Practice it:** Read your greeting aloud two or three times. Try a few practice runs with the voice mail system by recording it and erasing it until you get it flowing just right. Also, work the inflection of how you say words. A downward inflection at the end of a sentence gives your voice more authority and confidence.
- **Stand up and deliver it:** Your voice will sound stronger if you record your message standing up rather than sitting down. Standing helps you use your whole body to get the words out.
- **Do not mumble your messages:** Inhale, speak, throw your voice forward. Speech coaches encourage their clients to relax and take a few deep breaths before making speeches or delivering seminars. This sets up the voice and makes it work at its best. Before recording your greeting, inhale, begin to speak and send your voice forward, then make sure to open your mouth and let the sounds out. This will help bring out

your voice to the best tonal quality and make your words come out clearer.

- **Do it over until you get it right:** If at first you do not succeed, try again. On virtually every voice message system, you will get an unlimited number of tries to get your greeting perfect. Take your time and do it over until it is perfect.

Setting up a Company Greeting

If you are responsible for preparing the company (or workgroup) greeting, you will have a little more work to do. You will have to create the initial greeting that callers get when they try to reach your office and no one answers the phone.

You may record a greeting that is played as an automatic attendant all the time, or just during off hours. In either case, the same guidelines apply to a company greeting as a personal one. It should be short, friendly, and invite the caller into the company. It should encourage the caller to take action.

A company greeting should introduce the company then help the caller get to the proper extension. Depending on the way your voice messaging system is set up, all callers may have to pass through the initial greeting. In that case, it should be as short and informative as possible. It should offer help so that callers can maneuver around by themselves in order to complete their calls.

You will want to give the callers a few options. Among the options you should tell callers are: how to interrupt the greeting and get directly to an extension; give them instructions about how to transfer to an extension; help them find the company phone directory; or tell them how to leave a general message.

Sample Messages: Company Greeting

Here are two company greetings that you can use to get you started. Both cover the basics and invite the caller to take some action.

> *Thank you for calling ABC Company, Boston's largest housing development builders. If you are calling from a touch-tone phone and know your party's extension you can dial that now, or if you need a directory of numbers, you can dial 411. If you do not know your party's extension, would like to leave a general message, or are dialing from a rotary phone, you may hold on the line and begin recording your message at the tone. We will be happy to call you back. Thank you.*

This message both identifies and introduces the company, directs callers who know the right extension to place their calls, and offers alternatives. It is short, polite, to the point, and yet gets important information to the caller.

> *You have reached ABC Builders and Developers. Our office hours are from 8:00 A.M. until 5:00 P.M., Monday through Friday. If you are calling from a touch-tone phone and would like to leave a message, you can dial your party's extension now or at any time during this message. If you do not know your party's extension, you can press the star key on your telephone, then begin dialing the person's last name followed by first name until it is recognized. If you would like to leave a general message, or are dialing from a rotary phone, you may hold on the line and begin recording your message at the tone. We will be happy to call you back. Again, thank you for calling ABC Builders and Developers. Have a nice day.*

This message is a longer version than the first message, but gets the important points across early so that frequent callers do not have to spend a lot of time listening to information they do not need.

Leaving Voice Mail Messages

On the other side of the voice mail coin is the fine art of leaving good messages. Since getting communication and bits of information across is the goal, you should follow a few common-sense guidelines to make your messages effective.

- **Leave a meaningful message:** The worst message in the world goes something like this: *"Hi Ted, this is George. Please call me."* All you have accomplished with this message is to start the game of telephone tag. Poor Ted does not have a clue. He does not know if the company is still in business, if his house just burned up, or if he just won the state lottery. In fact, he does not even know where George is, and he might have to look up George's phone number if he does not have it already memorized.
- **Anticipate your message:** If you know that you might end up leaving voice mail rather than getting a real person on the line, plan out your message. You might even want to scratch down a couple of points so that you do not forget them when you start talking.
- **Do not forget to leave your return phone number:** Even if the person you are calling has your phone number, he or she might not have it with them. Since voice mail systems can be accessed from just about anywhere, the person could be out of town or running through an airport when he or she gets your message. Make it easy to call you back: Always leave your return phone number.
- **Leave your number last (last 8 seconds):** When you do leave your return phone number, be sure to leave it (or repeat it) in the end of your message. Many voice

mail systems let people rewind messages back just to the last eight seconds, and you will save the listener from having to hear all the details of your message before he or she calls you back. This is a small and subtle point, but certainly makes it more convenient for the listener to take the action you want—which is to return your call.

Managing Messages

Most voice mail systems let you take action on your messages once you have heard them. They let you save them, forward them, return them (if they originated within the system), or delete them.

But, do not let these options trick you into thinking that it is easy or convenient to manage voice mail. It is not.

For most systems, voice mail boxes are unmanageable. They do not let you save off many messages or organize them into projects or folders. At best, they give you one or two places to store them, and then do not let you recall them very efficiently. You cannot pick out messages from a voice mail list like most e-mail systems let you. Instead, you will have to go through them one at a time, until you get to the one you want.

When 'NOT' to use voice mail

Voice mail is for quick, non-detail-oriented information. It is also best used when you want to convey emotion. But, as good as it can be, it should not be used under certain circumstances.

- **Voice hammers:** Voice mail should never be used as a voice hammer. If you really get mad, count to 10, walk around your office, or pound on your desk. But, whatever you do, do not leave a voice mail message.

First of all, the person on the other end will not appreciate the non-personal scolding. It is a bad way to convey that kind of emotion.

Figure 5.9. Do not leave a voice message when you are upset.

Secondly, your voice mail could be saved and forwarded to anyone. Since voice mail records your actual voice, it is much more admissible in court than the same message sent by e-mail.

- **Details, details, details:** As we talked about earlier, voice mail is not the place to enumerate lots of details. It is certainly no place to list the 17 steps a person needs to take to improve his or her performance. That is an e-mail (or sometimes fax) document.

- **Confidential messages:** Use extreme caution when talking about confidential topics. People should not leave messages concerning the company layoffs, the unfriendly merger, or the payroll figures for Mary and Joe. If you never want to hear it again, do not say it on voice mail.

- **Talking about others:** It is never a good idea to talk about other people over voice mail—especially if the talk is negative. Telling someone about Harry's drinking habit or the boss's affair with the marketing department secretary is best left for real-time, unrecorded conversations. Since voice mail is so easy to forward, you never know when a message might fall into the wrong hands, or ears.

- **Do not leave flame mail:** Remember the "send" command on e-mail or voice mail is pretty permanent. If you leave a flame voice mail, it is almost impossible to remove it from the system. You may have thought things over and decided that was not the best move. Sorry, the message has been received at the other end.

Figure 5.10. Do not leave flaming voice mail.

DIRTY LITTLE TRICKS OF VOICE MAIL

Whether you choose to play them, or at least be aware of what other people do, you should know some of voice mail's dirty little tricks. While there are a host of tricks, these are among the most common:

- **Meeting avoidance:** Some people use voice mail when they do not want to have a face-to-face meeting or a two-way, real-time chat. While this is sometimes defensible, it is often the coward's way out. If you cannot look at someone in the face, go ahead, send a voice mail. It is better than having no communication at all.
- **Using the message date and time stamp:** Some people use the voice message date and time stamp in creative ways. Since most systems include the date and time stamp on every message, we know of people who play this to an advantage. For example, staffers

at an internal service department of a major corporation we know send voice mail message status updates only after 10:00 P.M. That way, they give the impression they are working well into the night on the client problem.

- **Sympathy voice mail:** Some people use their most pathetic voices to elicit sympathy with voice mail. Often this happens when the status report is not quite done, something broke or did not get fixed, or someone is looking for an extra favor.

- **Copying others on a voice message and not telling the receiver:** Be careful not to make assumptions that you are the only receiver of a message. Some people make a practice of copying others on voice mail, but not letting on.

- **Sending messages to 10, 20, or 50 people:** Messages may or may not need to be sent to groups, but some folks make a practice of it. While it is a good way to get information around in a hurry, copying up to 50 people on a message is sometimes a waste of time and disk space.

- **Leaving messages that cannot be forwarded:** Some systems, such as Skytalk, have a confidential tag that keeps the message from being forwarded. That can be used to the caller's advantage. But, before you use it, make sure that feature is active on the voice mail system.

TOMORROW'S VOICE MAIL TECHNOLOGY

Voice-processing technology is changing rapidly. Today's trend of computer-telephone integration will lead quickly into other types of technology partnering. Look for people to use integrated voice mail and e-mail systems, video conferencing, and other blended technologies.

Stand-alone voice mail systems have grown up and now possess almost every feature imaginable. There is not a lot of room for further innovation in voice-only systems.

Integrated voice and e-mail show a lot of promise. Already there are e-mail systems, such as those available for the Microsoft Windows environment, that let you add a voice message to any text file. This process, called *voice annotation*, is quickly capturing the imagination of workgroups as they need to pass both data and a few words explaining the data to each other.

Voice, video, text, and data are all coming together. As the chapters on video conferencing and e-mail will show, people are beginning to look at multimedia solutions. These powerful communication systems are poised to change the way we work, learn, and play. Stay tuned!

6

Portable Brains: Pagers, Phones, and PDAs

If you are a road warrior, you know you need connections. Dashing through airports and fumbling for pocket change to make calls from pay phones is no way to spend your business day.

Busy people need information to chase them, not the other way around. And, with today's plethora of portable and wireless technology, it is possible to cobble together links that let you stay in touch even while you are in transit. You can be here, there, and everywhere if you are willing to make some compromises and change some of your work habits.

Got a hot idea or an important question? If you can tap it into a chicklet-sized keyboard, you can send it to your colleagues around the world—instantly.

This chapter focuses on what is available from the world of pagers, cellular phones, and personal digital assistants (PDAs). It also provides you with a few tips on how to use these technologies so that they will indeed make you more productive. I will admit, these technologies are not for everyone. They are in various stages of maturity and no single product yet developed fills universal needs. So, if you are finding your business activities make you mobile, get ready to buy a box full of gadgets to keep you communicating. And, then, get ready to change some of your work habits and those of the people in your office.

Figure 6.1. Be prepared to buy a box full of these technologies to keep you communicating if you are mobile.

What? You say. Shouldn't the technology adapt to the way that I want to work? Of course, the answer is yes, but if you want to use the technology today, you must make the compromise. Otherwise, skip this chapter and come back to this topic in the year 2004. By then, the technology will be so sophisticated that it will read your mind.

WHAT IS A PORTABLE BRAIN ANYWAY?

Even though I use the term "portable brains" in this chapter, I would do just as well talking about electronic mouths and ears. After all, much of this technology is based on communicating information, not creating it.

Today's technology lets you take your knowledge base with you, and more importantly, lets information continue to flow even when you are out of the office.

Business people who purchase this technology usually have a goal of always wanting to stay in touch. They want to be available to customers, their office staff, or their boss—no matter what, 24 hours a day, 7 days a week, 365 days a year. Of course, there are some people who find this connectivity very invasive. They want a private life away from work. For these people, there is an "off" switch conveniently placed on each piece of portable technology.

Now, with that introduction (and caveat) said, let me start the tour of what is available with portable brains.

PAGERS

An easy and inexpensive way to stay in touch is to use a pager. Depending on how far you travel and what kind of information you need, you might only need to spend less than $10 a month on a paging service. That will give you a service supporting a single-line pager that can receive numerical pages only. And, even though this solution works for millions of people, it is like having someone send you Morse code if you try to do anything with it other than simply receive messages.

For more humanized uses (and a few dollars more), you can get a pager that displays several lines, text, or numbers.

Some services, such as PageNet and SkyTel, will send you broadcast messages and news summaries on the pager. PageNet's expanded service even goes one better; it beams in weather forecast, this day in history, market quotes, and even today's horoscopes. You will always feel in the know with your PageNet portable brain.

Better yet, PageNet's VoiceNow service (available in 1996) lets you receive and store voice messages from callers. You can play back messages at your convenience—it is like having an answering machine in your pocket. The service lets a caller record a short message, similar to voice mail. Then the system takes over and sends an alert to the VoiceNow, and then sends the message through thin air. The receiver stores messages on a digital chip inside the unit. You can listen to the message at your convenience, save it, and repeat it anytime until you delete it. It holds four minutes worth of recording, which is enough for about twenty average length phone messages (assuming your callers are reasonable people, not Chatty Charlie and Chatty Cathy).

Options for Pagers

If you are shopping for a pager, try to figure out your specific needs first. Generally speaking, the more you travel, the more features and services you will want from the pager and paging service. Hard core road warriors should not feel shy about getting the souped-up version of a pager—after all, you will probably spend more time with it than your spouse.

Figure 6.2. Pick the souped-up version of your favorite pager—you will probably spend more time with it than your spouse.

The following check list should help you figure out what services you need, and what kind of pager to buy or rent.

Service Feature	Options
Service Range	Local or regional National International
Type of Message	Numeric only Text and numbers Voice
Broadcast	Receive e-mail Receive text messages Receive news summaries Receive stock quotes (customized or by industry category) Receive weather, horoscopes, or other information Receive voice message
Fax	Receive notice of a fax (that is stored by the paging service that you can retrieve by a fax machine later)

Table 6.1. Check list for pager needs.

As for the paging device itself, you have got other options to choose from. Most pagers offer a clock feature and several alert options. When your pager receives a message, it can make a chirping sound until you view the message, emit just one short chirp, simply vibrate, or send no alert (it just waits for you to look at it).

Depending on the memory available in your pager, most pagers let you save up to 16 or 20 messages. Some pagers let you lock a message, giving you an extra measure of protection so you will not inadvertently delete a message.

Overall, pagers are handy devices to let people stay in touch with you. You can get a service to reach you almost anywhere. One caveat, you cannot talk back. For now, pagers are one-way devices. They only receive. This is good enough for many business needs, but sometimes calls for supplements, like having a cell phone or wireless e-mail nearby.

Tips for Using Pagers

If you put on your thinking cap, you will see that pagers can do a lot more than just send a number to people.

- **Use alerts and alarms.** Some pagers offer alarm functions so they can double for a travel alarm when you

Figure 6.3. Use your pager as an alarm.

are on the road. (It never hurts to have a backup in case the hotel operator forgets your wakeup call.) The alarm feature can also be used to keep you on time for your next appointment.

- **Tell the time at home.** Most pagers have a clock function. If you are traveling across time zones, leave your pager set to your hometown time and reset your wrist watch to the local time. That way you will not get confused and you will always know what time it is at home.

- **De-list your number.** Do not put your pager phone number on your business card *unless* you want everyone to know it (and I do mean everyone, including Chatty Charlie who will call you to let you know each time he steps down the hall to grab a cup of coffee). If you publish your pager number, do not complain when people use it for unimportant messages.

- **Get text and numbers.** If you get a lot of pages, get an alphanumeric pager so people can send you messages. It is highly disturbing to get a page every ten minutes, then hunt for a phone to return a call, only to find out that the message was to let you know someone showed up early.

- **Create codes.** If you did not heed my tip above, and you only have a numeric pager, set up some codes with your office staff and family. Some people create "urgency" codes that they append to their phone numbers, such as:

111   call when you can
511   call quickly
911   emergency, call immediately

- **Install software on office PCs.** If you have an alphanumeric pager (one that displays both text and numbers) and your paging service has software for people to type in messages from a PC, give a copy to your kids at home. It is fun for children to type a note to Mommy or Daddy.
- **Shake don't wake.** Get in the habit of switching your pager to vibrate only before you go into meetings,

Figure 6.4. Set your pager to vibrate when you need quiet time.

business presentations, or other public places. Neither your boss nor your fellow meeting attendees appreciate the disruption of a chirping pager at an inopportune moment.

CELLULAR PHONES

While 1960s TV audiences were mesmerized by Maxwell Smart's phone (in his shoe), today business people think that a shoe phone would be too big and clunky. With featherweight phones, such as the six-and-a-half ounce Nokia 232, that measures less than six inches in length, it is hard to imagine phones shrinking anymore.

NOKIA 232

Figure 6.5. The easiest and most versatile cellular phones are featherweight and small, like this 6.5-ounce Nokia 232. You can take it anywhere!

Cellular phones have become the constant companion of many busy business people. Sales of new phones and cellular service continue to grow, reaching $14.4 billion in 1994, according to Northern Business Information, a unit for Datapro Information Services. The report, "World Cellular Network Equipment Markets: 1994/1995 Edition," notes that cellular providers are enjoying more liberal government regulations and lower equipment costs.

These conditions set the environment for greater competition, lower costs, and more services. So get ready; over the next few years a lot of voice and data traffic will be flying through the air.

Options for Cellular Phones and Service

If you are shopping for your first or fifteenth cellular phone, you will undoubtedly get confused by the dizzying array of shapes and sizes. To pick the unit that is right for you, you need to do a little thinking about what and how you intend to use your cell phone. Do not be lulled into the next "free phone" offer only to find that you have selected a phone that is too heavy or cumbersome for your needs.

Here is a list of considerations for your cellular phone shopping:

Product Feature	Options	Considerations
Weight	Cell phones weigh in anywhere from 6 to 16 ounces.	Generally lightweight phones are more expensive but the extra cost is worth it if you need to carry the phone in your pocket or purse.
Size	Most phones range between 6 and 10 inches in length and 1 to 2 inches in thickness	Like weight, smaller is better and more expensive. If you want portability, go for the smallest and thinnest that you can get. One exception, if you have a large hand, you might find the super small units uncomfortable.
Battery life	From 30-minute talk time with 8-hour standby to 150-minutes talk and 32-hour standby.	Most phones offer a range of battery options that extend your talk time and standby time. If you spend much time in a car you can supplement your battery with a fast-charging cigarette lighter adapter.

Table 6.2. Check List for cellular phone needs.

Product Feature	Options	Considerations
Signal strength	From .6 watts to 3.0 watts	If you travel mostly in metropolitan areas, a phone with .6 watts will do fine. If your travel takes you in and out of different areas, look for a booster that will give you better signal strength while in your car.
Programmable keys	From 4 to 99 programmed keys for 1-key dialing to frequent numbers	Many phones offer speed-dial capabilities so you can store frequently called numbers in the phone's memory. This feature may or may not be important to you. In reality, most people rarely use more than four or five speed dial numbers.
Special adapters	Hands-free desktop units; hands-free car units; PCMCIA adapters (for portable computers)	Depending on your needs, you may or may not require add-on adapters. If you do, make sure your phone supports these adapters.

Table 6.2. Continued.

Tips for Using Cellular Phones

Cellular phones have taken the world of business communications by storm. They are, however, different from your conventional corded desk phone. Cell phones lack total privacy, are expensive to use, and can run out of battery life at the most inopportune moment. Here are a few tips to keep you talking straight and clear with cellular:

- **Don't say anything you would not tell your grandmother.** Cellular phone conversations are not secure.

Low-cost scanning devices can easily pick up your conversation, your phone number, as well as all the phone numbers that you dial. Unless you know you are on a special restricted frequency (and you work for the Secret Service) you should assume everything you say is being broadcast over the radio.

- **Don't publish your cellular phone number.** Most cellular services charge for incoming calls so if you must publish a mobile number, give people your pager number. That way you can call back people who you want and not pay air time listening to the town gossip. Even for those all-important office calls, it is best to ask your fellow workers to call your pager and leave a message. Then, you can decide whether you should call back on your cellular phone or another phone. (Since cellular roaming charges cost upwards of $1.00 a minute, it is best to reserve the service for when there is no other phone available.)

- **Avoid traffic accidents, get a hands-free unit.** If you drive a lot and talk on your cell phone, get a hands-free unit installed. For as little as $150, you will never again have to maneuver into weird contortions trying to balance the steering wheel, the phone, and your shoulder.

Figure 6.6. Get a hands-free unit to avoid traffic accidents.

- **Join the spare battery club.** If your travels take you to places where you cannot easily recharge, then carry a spare (charged) battery with you. For extended travel, keep it in your suitcase if you do not have room in a briefcase or purse.

- **Avoid a meltdown.** If you leave your phone in a parked car, keep it out of direct sunlight. High temperatures can shorten battery life, damage electrical components, and melt plastic.
- **Watch your roaming.** If you find yourself roaming into the same area frequently, check to see if you can avoid the surcharges by buying an extended service. Also, some cellular phones allow you to program in two local numbers so you can have a local number for Boston and another one for Chicago.
- **End a call when it crackles.** All cellular systems have certain areas where the service breaks up and causes a lot of static on the line. If you experience this problem, it is best to end the call and replace later. Nobody wants the sound of crackling. Also, if you know of an area in your town with bad service (probably having lots of trees or high electrical wires), avoid using the phone while you drive through.
- **Review your bill.** It is a good idea to get the detailed billing service from your cellular service and review it each month. Cellular crooks are plentiful and sometimes clever. They can easily deposit a few extra calls on your bill.
- **Turn your phone off before plane rides.** The FAA and your battery will appreciate the rest. Cellular phones can interfere with the aircraft's systems. Besides, over 10,000 feet, cellular does not work consistency. It is doubtful you could establish a crystal-clear connection. You will also conserve your battery by turning the phone off completely.

Figure 6.7. Always turn your cellular phone completely off when riding in an airplane.

PDAs

The personal digital assistant (PDA) takes business connectivity to new unprecedented levels. Today's units, when hooked to wireless communications networks, can deliver mail, news, and most importantly, let you send back a response—all with the click of a few keys.

Do you need to dash off a quick note to the office while you are in a taxi? Or, how about catching up on reading and responding to your e-mail during a long plane ride? Do you want instant alerts with the industry news or stock market quotes? Or, how about getting an early start on your status report? You can do all this with a PDA.

SONY.   MAGIC LINK™ PERSONAL COMMUNICATOR

Figure 6.8. Sony's Magic Link PDA offers features that give you a portable desktop.

Of course, of all the technology I have talked about so far, the diminutive PDA is potentially the most invasive as well as the most empowering to your lifestyle. Not everyone wants yet another device that can find them when they are watching the kids' basketball game, beep them in church, or forward e-mail when they are walking through a meadow. Not everyone wants to be found all of the time.

For those of us who do not mind, then the future looks bright for gaining productivity benefits by using PDAs, with one caveat: Do not expect these units to turn into your single source of information or communication. They are not appendages.

During my research for this book, I talked with many people disappointed that PDAs did not meet their expectations. When I asked why, almost universally, the displeased users cited that they expected to free themselves of other electronic gizmos once they started using a

PDA. Nice idea, but it just does not work that way. The PDA is supplemental technology; it rarely displaces other computers. Instead, it displaces paper, like your notebook, DayTimer, and address book.

So, if you think that you can abandon other electronic paraphernalia, like your cell phone, pager, notebook computer or desktop computer, then stop right now. Take a breather, walk around the block, grab a cup of coffee, watch TV (but no science fiction), and resume reading later. You need time to come to your senses.

Options for PDAs

After a few trials and failures, today's crop of PDAs is beginning to show real promise. Some, like Sony's Magic Link, use sophisticated operating systems that give you a set of desktop-like features. PDAs come with or without built-in keyboards and many let you just point to a button or icon on the screen to launch a program.

For example, General Magic's MagicCap operating system, which the Sony PDA uses, lets you set up an electronic Rolodex, e-mail, inbox, outbox, and calendar. To use any of the programs, you need only to tap on the screen. The pictures on its screen are so intuitive that even a non-computer-literate person can navigate around the system easily. And, if there is something that you need help with, the Magic Link offers a robust on-board help system so you do not have to carry around tons of manuals.

Hewlett-Packard's HPLX200 Palmtop computer has more than two million units in existence and doubles as a pocket secretary. It can be coupled with a modem, or radio modem and e-mail software to give you wireless e-mail.

I have been carrying around this type of setup—a palmtop with an Ericsson MobiDEM (wireless modem), and RadioMail, an Internet connected wireless e-mail for nearly three years. It runs over the RAM Mobile data network, which is a packet radio network. (It is not cellular, but it is a close cousin technology-wise.) For me, it has been a great way to stay in touch and pass around information when I am on the go. And, I have sent mail from some of the strangest places like moving sidewalks in airports, taxicabs, car rental counters, and a few other places. What I have learned from the experience: People can cheat the clock. I can steal away time that normally would be dead space in my day and eke out a productive moment.

That gets me back to PDAs. For business purposes, PDAs are useless if they do not communicate. If you do not have effective communications and file-transfer capability, you will find yourself rekeying information back and forth between multiple computers. (And we call this progress!)

Take stock of your expectations before buying a PDA. Ask yourself what you expect to do. Imagine spending a day with the unit. What will you do with it? Who needs to see the information you created?

Then, as you make your purchase plans, make sure you are equipped with proper connections so you can exchange information with your colleagues at the office or with your own personal computer.

Here are a few considerations for picking out the PDA that is perfect for you:

Product Feature	Options	Considerations
Weight	PDAs weigh in anywhere from 3 to 8 pounds.	Weight frequently correlates with features. Light units generally do not have much power or expandability. Unless you need to carry the PDA in your pocket or purse, you will probably compromise weight for added capabilities.

Table 6.3. Check list for purchasing a PDA.

Product Feature	Options	Considerations
Size	Most PDAs range between 6″ and 8″ in length, 4″ to 6″ are wide, and are about 1″ thick.	Like weight, smaller often means less functional. Even so, today's full function units, usually measure less than 6 X 6 inches.
Battery life	From 8 hours to two days.	Most PDAs use regular AA batteries, NiCad batteries or a combination of both.
Keyboards	No keyboard, onscreen keyboard, chicklet-sized keyboard, port for keyboard	Try the keyboard and do not depend on a pen. Since pen computing cannot accurately decipher most people's handwriting, the keyboard is still a requirement. Make sure you can tolerate it.
Communications	None, telephone jack (RJ-11 plug), infrared device, wireless support	Many PDAs contain an infrared port for local file transfer. For long distances, you will need a telephone modem or packet radio modem to transfer information.
PCMCIA or PC Card slot	None, Type II, or Type III slot	A PC Card slot (sometimes called PCMCIA) is important to add memory, disk storage, or special communications capabilities. Your PDA should have at least one Type II slot.

Table 6.3. Continued.

Tips for Using PDAs

PDAs are technology that you will want to have with you at all times. Consider it your traveling companion. Here are a few tips for the care and feeding of your PDA.

- **When it comes to batteries, carry a spare.** While most PDAs have good battery life, they will not go for days of constant use. It is a good idea to add a spare battery to your suit case or carry on bag. Do not depend on the all-night drugstore to stock what you need.

- **Carry small attachments in a see-through bag.** PDAs are small; their attachments are smaller! Avoid hassles looking for an adapter or memory card and put all the attachments in a see-through bag. It makes life a lot easier if you know where to look.

- **Back up, back up, BACK UP!** PDA's convenient on-off features seem so convenient that many people forget they risk losing files. You never know when something can go awry, like inadvertently erasing all the files in your checkbook program. Save yourself the hassle and develop a regular backup routine. You do not have to back up everything. Select the most important files and either transfer them to another computer or store copies on a memory card.

- **Work up file transfer procedures.** Many people complain that their secretary keeps information on one set of files while they use another. If that is your problem, you can partially solve it with procedures. Look for software, like LapLink, that will help you synchronize your files on multiple computers. Make sure you and your staff know how to update your files.

- **Don't freeze or fry your PDA.** Like other sensitive electronic equipment, you will not want to subject your PDA to extreme temperature conditions. It is best to keep the unit in a carry case or your briefcase. Also, be aware—direct prolonged periods of direct sunlight can harm the screen.

WHAT'S NEXT: COMPUTERS IN YOUR POCKET

Portable-brain technology, stemming from today's pagers, cellular phones, and PDAs, will continue to unfold. Do not be surprised to see the next generation come with eyeglasses, earphones, data gloves, and a small central processing unit designed to fit in your pocket.

As multiple technologies converge, I expect to see a combo-TV set, cell phone, wireless e-mail device with data gloves instead of a keyboard. You will someday (hopefully soon) be able to don your information appliance, focus your glasses, and tap into a library, read the local news, or see coverage of the big sports event.

Moreover, you will be able to tune in any time and from any place. The factors of time, space, and location will become meaningless in a world where information surrounds and follows us.

7

Energize Your Message with E-mail

For many business people today, electronic mail (e-mail) is the best invention since the wheel—maybe even better. Legions of business people have already found e-mail the single most important part of today's information technology, and others eventually will. Progressive business managers recognize its power quickly, and come to use e-mail more than any single other information technology application—more than spreadsheets, word processors, graphics application, or databases.

Why? Because e-mail can make moving information from here to there a lot faster as well as a lot easier. E-mail, more than other technologies combines the power of computers and communications. It can move information and knowledge over, under, around, and through an organization with lightning speed.

E-mail often picks up where other technologies stop. Unlike voice mail, e-mail lets you easily add detail and complexity to the message. Unlike fax, data contained in e-mail messages can be electronically stored and easily reused.

E-mail's reach into our business and personal lives continues to spread. Wireless messaging technology, introduced in 1992, opened up still another dimension.

With wireless e-mail, this follows the person to wherever he or she goes. You do not have to go looking for e-mail; it will find you. You can carry your own personal e-mail voice and ear as easily as you can carry a small book. Products like RadioMail and WyndMail, the first commercial wireless e-mail products, provide extraordinary freedom and mobility because you

Figure 7.1. Work or play, wireless e-mail can follow you to almost any location.

can simply carry the unit—and your mail finds you. No matter what city, what time of day, just turn on the unit and your e-mail magically appears.

But, alas, e-mail's benefits are not always seen or known before it is used. Many a corporate executive who once winced at the thought of e-mail, had turned full circle to find it is the most widely used computer application in the company. Better yet, e-mail has enormous cultural effects that help flatten our hierarchical management structures. It lets people cut though the corporation and move information quickly from one place to another.

E-mail is big business. According to some experts there are 30 to 40 million e-mail boxes already installed somewhere on planet Earth. And, more are on the way.

Figure 7.2. E-mail can reach you any place on earth.

For those of us who use it, e-mail surely changes what, when, and how we communicate. It also changes expectations for immediacy. Would you expect an instant answer to a written letter or memo? Probably not, because the logistics of moving the document from one place to another take too long. With e-mail, however, this is not only possible, but sometimes expected. In some situations, you can even type messages back and forth simultaneously and get nearly instant feedback.

E-mail is exciting. And this chapter is designed to chart the way. I am going to take a winding tour through the nuances of e-mail starting with a definition. Then I will share some insight about how e-mail changes the way people communicate and sometimes changes the corporate culture itself. Then, I will move into more practical territory with a discussion of how to make the best of e-mail, what you should expect from an e-mail system, and some tips on running it. In case you have missed out on some of the fun so far, I will even introduce some ways to put emotion into e-mail with "earth." These are the little symbols that resemble facial expressions for smiling, frowning, winking, and other emotions. Finally, if you were unlucky enough to be given the job of setting up your company's e-mail, I will share some important tips for selecting the right package for you. But, first, let's start with the basics of what e-mail is and how it transforms people and organizations.

WHAT IS E-MAIL?

E-mail is best thought of as an electronic method of moving information from one person to another. Information is generated by another person, or sometimes by a computer. It is like conventional mail, but its potential reach is much broader.

Sometimes there is confusion about where e-mail starts and stops. There are actually several technologies that get caught in the definition web, they include: e-mail, which is person-to-person(s) messaging; groupware, which lets many co-workers (or workgroups) share information with each other in a collaborative effort; public forums, which are like computerized bulletin boards for different people to share information; and on-line databases, which let people communicate directly with data stored somewhere on a computer.

For the sake of argument, we will stick to person-to-person e-mail messaging in this chapter. I will cover groupware in Chapter 8. We will spend time with extended versions like public forums and on-line databases in later chapters.

From a mechanical standpoint, e-mail closely follows the metaphor of regular mail. If you look at the way e-mail is packaged and handled, many of the familiar functions are duplicated, such as addressing, sorting, and delivering. With e-mail, only computers (instead of people) do most of the work.

For example, each person on an e-mail system will have his or her own address and mailbox. Messages intended for that person are delivered to the mailbox and are held until collected. The e-mail system, in essence, stores and then forwards messages.

Many of the newer e-mail products provide expanded features. Aside from simply receiving and passing on messages, these products let you attach files to messages. These files can be common data files such as spreadsheets, word-processing documents, or they can even contain voice or video clips.

Figure 7.3. Like the paper-oriented postal service, most e-mail packages put an envelope around your message and use a carrier to deliver it to your mailbox. The difference is that e-mail does it all by computer. Look Ma, no hands.

Other conveniences have become popular, such as the ability to forward mail to other people; courtesy copy someone on a message; get a return receipt when someone opens mail you sent; or the option of storing mail in folders after you have read it.

E-mail Versus "The Old Fashioned Way"

Let's look at a stark reality, the old way versus the electronically empowered way. If you are a corporate citizen in a large organization (or even some small ones) and you want to get a piece of information to the guy down the hall, you might have to go through hoops and loops to accomplish it.

Take, for example, one major Fortune 100 company's official procedure for sending a report to a coworker down the hall. Believe it or not; this policy existed up until just a few years ago. It involved a 16-step process that went something like this:

Before E-mail	After E-mail
Step 1: Business person hand writes a memo or report on a yellow writing tablet; gives it off to his or her secretary.	Step 1: Business person drafts own document in a word processing program, or directly in the e-mail software.
Step 2: Secretary proofs the document and edits for spelling, grammar, and correct use of company trademarks.	Step 2: Business person does spell check and sends electronic document to guy down the hall and electronically files a draft copy.
Step 3: Secretary walks the memo and deposits it into the wire basket in front of the word-processing center.	Step 3: Guy down the hall gets message.
Step 4: The center clocks in the document, assigns a job number to it, and puts it in the queue for the next available word-processing specialist.	
Step 5: The word-processing specialist types the document in draft form and places it in the out basket.	
Step 6: Secretary collects the document, proofs it, places editing marks on it, and returns it for approval to the business person.	

Table 7.1. Sixteen-step procedure versus three-step process.

Before E-mail	After E-mail
Step 7: Business person reviews the draft, edits it if necessary, and returns it to the secretary.	
Step 8: Secretary copies the marked-up draft, returns it to the word-processing center for final edits, corrections, and printing.	
Step 9: Word-processing center clocks in the document, assigns a job number to it and puts it in the queue for the next available specialist.	
Step 10: Word-processing specialist retrieves the file, makes the appropriate edits, prints it in final form, and places it in the out basket.	
Step 11: Secretary picks up completed document, proofs it again and gives it to the business person for signature.	
Step 12: Business person signs document and returns it to secretary.	
Step 13: Secretary copies document, files it, addresses an inter-office envelope and sends it to the mail room.	
Step 14: Mail room receives envelope, sorts it, and distributes it in the next mail run.	

Table 7.1. Continued

Before E-mail	After E-mail
Step 15: Secretary of the guy down the hall receives mail, opens envelope and places it in appropriate folder, and delivers mail.	
Step 16: Person down the hall gets message.	
Total elapsed time: 3 days to 1 week.	Total elapsed time: 3–5 minutes to an hour (depending on the sender's typing skills).

Table 7.1. Continued.

This is not a joke (or even a slight exaggeration). It was company policy—the rules, the law. The same procedure was followed for everything from a one-page memo to a 200-page report. No exceptions allowed. There were even administrators employed in each department to make sure no one violated or short-circuited the ordained company procedures. (In fact, when the first personal computers came into this company, there was a major management and political confrontation trying to stop business people from using PCs to write their own memos.)

Now contrast the sixteen-step procedure with the way things are done today with e-mail. Today, the process of getting information to the guy down the hall can be as little as three steps. And, depending on the sender's typing skills, the whole transaction can take place in as little as three minutes.

Moreover, today's approach does not cost more than the old system did even when you consider all the costs for computer hardware and software.

Changing Cultures

E-mail, once it is embraced by an organization, can change the organization's culture. Look at the example I just mentioned. The company went from a sixteen-step one-week lag time to a three-step, near-instant mode of getting information from one place to another. Considering just the speed difference alone, you would expect some kind of change.

Frequently, the changes ushered in by e-mail come in the form of changing the tone, formality, length and distribution list of messages. Take tone and formality. As people begin to use e-mail more frequently, they tend to make the tone of their messages friendlier. Since e-mail dialogs suffer from not being able to convey a facial expression or voice change, people find ways of compensating for it by changing the wording, or tone. Also, e-mail, among seasoned users, is far less formal than letterhead-based memos.

Figure 7.4. Make the tone of your e-mail message friendly.

E-mail messages tend to be short and to the point. While there are no written rules of e-mail etiquette, many organizations develop their own style, which then begins to change the culture of the organization.

Some researchers in the field also believe that e-mail encourages another form of communication up and down the organization. Rank and title seem to have less importance on e-mail messages. Likewise, e-mail shows no gender, racial, or appearance bias. Messages look the same, and readers tend to focus on content, not the looks of the person creating the message.

There is also evidence that e-mail tends to encourage otherwise shy or introverted people to speak up and contribute. Since there is no fear of instant rejection with comments or facial expressions, shy people are sometimes more willing to express opinions over e-mail than they are in person.

Finally, e-mail tends to change the order and number of people on distribution lists. Since it is so easy to add another name to a distribution list, many people freely send courtesy copies of e-mail out. This encourages sharing, but sometimes over-does a situation.

How Organizations Change with E-mail

While there have not been reams of definitive research on how e-mail changes organizational behavior, most people agree that it does. They use words like: empowerment, flattened organizations, better and faster messaging. Over all, most organizations find e-mail a good experience.

Of the observations worth noting, I like the one about how people change the way they refer to e-mail. As organizations develop more mature users, e-mail goes from being a foreign substance, to a part of the every day activity.

E-mail Pitfalls

Even with e-mail's ease of use and the great promise for improved productivity, there are pitfalls. E-mail can be under-used, overused, and otherwise abused.

Sometimes people get so wrapped up in the power of e-mail they begin to over use it or hide behind it and neglect responsibilities for more personal communication. While e-mail can replace face-to-face or telephone discussions, it should not take the place of *all* discussions.

Also, it is important to be sensitive to the skill level and e-mail maturity of the people you interact with. You may have jumped in with both feet to the electronically empowering world of e-mail, but some of your correspondents may not have. For example, we know of one government contract that was not awarded to the e-mail-addicted incumbent. It turns out that when e-mail was installed at the contractor, he no longer felt it necessary

Figure 7.5. Just like sending a barrage of paper memos, some people hide behind their e-mail rather than have face-to-face chats.

to call on the client personally. The contractor began to send everything by e-mail, thinking it was more efficient. The client did not exactly feel the same way.

Meaningless Mail

Some people find e-mail as a great place to generate meaningless mail. Since e-mail is so fast and easy to use, some people tend to abuse it. They insist on recording their every impression, their every activity, and their every emotion.

Meaningless mail is all right in a small organization where there are not too many people generating messages without merit. But, in large organizations, or in places where there are many meaningless mail generators, somebody should take action.

The best way to fix meaningless mail is to tell the perpetuator (tactfully) about it. Sometimes these people are so enamored with the technology, they simply do not know it. Ask to be taken off the distribution list, and tell the person why. In most cases he or she will get the hint and probably slow it down for other victims.

Copies and Copy Lists

I know people who have huge distribution lists and forward each and every e-mail they receive right back out again to legions of colleagues and co-workers. That does not always make sense. It sometimes makes an e-mail message from "Harry" less important to read.

For example, recently a few corporate workers exchanged some words about not being up-to-date on a project. One commented, "Well, Sam, I sent you that information in an e-mail." And Sam fired back, "Joe, you send me twenty-five e-mails a day. How am I supposed to know the important ones?"

Bad Writer Syndrome

There is no place in the e-mail world for bad writers. If you (or one of your colleagues) cannot put thoughts

down in an organized way, e-mail is going to be painful. We have seen bad writer syndrome work as a real disadvantage to the individual. Since the person has problems organizing his or her thoughts, it turns out that he or she does not use e-mail (or sends out very long and boring messages that nobody reads).

Figure 7.6. If you are a bad writer, you better get some help. E-mail will only get your garbled message there faster.

Check out our tips later in this chapter for advice on creating better messages. If you still need help, consider going to a course at a vocational school or local community college. Perhaps, if you work in a large organization, you can even convince the corporate training department that this is a topic to include on the company training list.

TIPS FOR HOW TO USE E-MAIL

Everyone develops a special e-mail style. Most people find that e-mail correspondence is short, informal, and very direct. We have assembled some tips for making the most out of your e-mail exchanges. They include:

- **Top-down writing.** Write short messages with the most important points in the very beginning. Most e-mail messages are less than three paragraphs, but be sure to put the most important part of the message in the first paragraph.
- **Careful copying.** Do not copy everyone including your grandmother on every e-mail message. Use care when building a huge distribution list—you will waste everyone's time trying to deal with mountains of messages they have no interest in.

Figure 7.7. You can bury your co-workers in e-mail if you are not careful.

- **User folders.** If your e-mail system supports it, maintain a group of project- or people-related folders to save your messages. This will help you maintain the system and keep the in box from growing out of control.

- **Don't be afraid to delete.** Some e-mail messages are not that important. They do not need to be saved for eternity in your in box or a folder. Delete them after they have fulfilled their purpose.
- **Watch fast-forwarding.** While it is generally all right to forward a person's message to another, be careful when you do it. We know of cases where messages containing negative comments about a person were forwarded directly to the person. It was embarrassing for everyone involved.
- **Create short meaningful messages.** You do not need to write your own version of *War and Peace* with each e-mail message. Make it short and to the point, without omitting important information, of course. Unless you have a lot to say, make most of your e-mail messages short—a paragraph or two.
- **Include copies.** If you are replying to a message, include a copy of the original message (or at least, some words of that message) so that the person will remember what you are talking about. It is all to easy to forget the original message and subsequently scramble the meaning.
- **Don't be a mail stuffer—watch your copy lists.** A common mistake of well-meaning e-mail enthusiasts is to create big distribution lists of people, and then copy them on every possible message. While e-mail is an effective way to bring lots of information to lots of people, it can also drown them in too much trivia.

- **Check e-mail three times a day (or more)!** Your e-mail will not work any faster than the Pony Express if

Figure 7.8. Check your e-mail at least three times a day.

you do not check it often. People who only look at their e-mail once a week or so defeat the purpose of having it. A good routine is to check for mail in the morning, at lunch time, and before you leave for the day. Another option, for people who use advanced operating environments like Microsoft Windows, is to keep your e-mail system up and running all day long. That way, when a message comes in for you, you will be alerted right away.

- **Forward or share your mail.** If you cannot check your mail early and often, consider forwarding it to someone who can. Many e-mail systems allow you to forward your mail to another user. Then when something comes in that you need to respond to, that person can let you know. This is not quite as good as being there personally, but it sure beats leaving mail in your mailbox for weeks.

- **Don't leave them hanging—reply promptly.** Most people expect a response to an e-mail message the same day. In some organizations, it is permissible to hold up on a response for a day or two, but slow responses tend to defeat the benefits of e-mail.

If you do not have a full answer to an e-mail inquiry, and need some extra time, be sure to let the person at the other end know. A simple message back, saying *"Stand by, George, I will need to research that issue for you"* will help keep your e-mail correspondent informed.

- **Don't flame.** Some e-mail messages will undoubtedly evoke emotion—either because they touch on a sensitive subject, or because you misunderstood them. Be careful not to fan the fire with a quick and curt response back.

Always take a second look at the original message before responding. Then, only respond when you are not acting emotionally to the message.

E-MAIL SHORTHAND AND EMOTICONS

Early e-mail users invented some clever ways of making up for not being able to convey emotion. Since you cannot change the inflection of your voice, nor your body language inside an e-mail document, people have developed other methods of sending emotion within the text.

There are two common methods, *acronyms* and *emoticons*. People use shorthand symbols, or *acronyms*, to say certain key phrases.

Originally, e-mail shorthand was used to spare the typist from having to key in lots of characters—and to spare the computer systems from having to use up all its expensive disk space. Now, it is used by people as a convenience.

E-mail Acronyms

Most e-mail *acronyms* are easy to figure out. For example, a common e-mail shorthand term is *BTW*, which stands for *by the way*. Another one, which conveys some humor and emotion is *ROFL,* which stands for *rolling on the floor laughing.* Table 7.2 gives you an abridged list of some of the more common acronyms. More extensive listings of e-mail acronyms are sometimes printed in PC-oriented magazines or available from public on-line subscription services, such as CompuServe or America On-line.

Using Acronyms

E-mail acronyms can be used at any point in a message. For the most part they are capitalized and begin a sentence. For example, you might read:

> *FWIW, I'm going to take off the week of December 12th for vacation. If you have anything that you need to cover with me, make sure you contact me by December 9th. Thanks.*

In this message, FWIW stands for *for what it's worth.* Notice, it saved a few extra characters of typing.

Acronym	Meaning
AFK	Away from keyboard
BAK	Back at keyboard
BRB	Be right back
BTW	By the way
FWIW	For what it's worth
FAS	For a second
FYI	For your information
FAW	For a while
GD&R	Grinning, ducking, and running
GMTA	Great minds think alike
IMHO	In my humble opinion
IOW	In other words

Table 7.2. Common e-mail acronyms.

Acronym	Meaning
LOL	Laughing out loud
ROTF	Rolling on the floor (laughing)
TTFN	Tata for now!
WB	Welcome back
WTG	Way to go!

Table 7.2. Continued.

E-MAIL-EMOTICOMS

Emoticons are specially contrived symbols that are supposed to resemble a facial expression. Unlike e-mail acronyms, which are easy to figure out, *emoticons* take a little getting used to. It helps to tilt your head to the left to see them right-side-up.

> An example: **:-)**

In this example, if you tilt your head correctly, you will see two eyes and a mouth. Now, let's see if I can make the emoticon wink.

> A wink: **;-)**

Some of the more common *emoticons* are shown in Table 7.3. See if you can easily recognize the expression.

Emoticon	Meaning
:-)	a smile
;-)	a smile with a wink
*<:-)	face with a party hat
:-D	a big smile
:-(	a frown
:`-(	crying
:-X	not saying a word
:-o	a look of wonderment
:-p	sticking out tongue
>:-)	a devilish face

Table 7.3. Common emoticons

Emoticon	Meaning
O:-	an angelic face
:-/	a perplexed look
[]	a hug
:-*	a kiss
---===[}	a flung pie
[-U	a mug
Y	a wineglass
~~	waves
@@	rolling your eyes
:-$	put your money where your mouth is
B-)	wears glasses
B:-)	wears sunglasses on head
:-|	a smoker
(:-D	someone has a big mouth
:-)'	tends to drool

Table 7.3. Continued.

For the very uninitiated, both acronyms and emoticons can be confusing. Make sure that your reader knows them, or has access to a handy list before you start using them in your messages. A good idea, if you wish to introduce this shorthand into an organization, is to publish a reference list and keep it current. The list should be online and easy for other people using the e-mail system to get.

E-MAIL DO'S AND DON'TS

Here is a list of some important things to remember when you are working with e-mail:

- **DO write enough detail in your notes to give your reader a complete message.** Most e-mail messages are short—less than four lines. Make sure they have meaning. Be sure there is enough information for the receiver to respond to or you will be bouncing back and forth several messages just to clarify the point. If you are writing a page or more, create the note on a word processor so you can spell check and grammar check the note before you send it in e-mail.

- **DO read your e-mail note carefully before you send it.** Watch your sentence structure. Use short sentences and avoid using too much slang.

- **DO write in a direct and informative style.** Provide all the necessary answers to questions like: Who? What? Where? When? Why? and sometimes How? Often you may describe events or problems so you will want to use the past tense when events have already occurred. You should shift into the present or future tense when you want to tell your reader something is happening now or will take place in the future.

- **DON'T forget to respond to your e-mail messages and notes promptly.** As a matter of courtesy, you should check your e-mail in-basket at least two or three times a day and attempt to immediately respond to those messages needing action. Even if you do not have the information your correspondent asks for, send a reply to the request and let the person know that you are researching the question or problem and that you plan to return with an answer by a specified date. In this way, your clients, boss, or co-workers will not wonder whether you received and understood their note.

- **DON'T send flame mail.** Sending off an emotionally charged e-mail message or note is something that you will possible regret.

    Shut down your computer, take a walk around the office, go to lunch, take a coffee break. Chill out. DO try to make up some questions you can ask the correspondent who caused you to become angry or anxious. Questions can clarify the originator's message and often defuse a rash of angry exchanges. Think about what you write. Would your boss (or your mother) approve of your action?

- **DON'T type your e-mail in ALL CAPS.** It is like shouting and it is very difficult to read. You can use all caps for emphasis on occasion, or put an asterisk on either side of the word you are trying to emphasize. See the examples that follow and see how the second and third example get the message across without hurting the readers eyes:

Figure 7.9. Don't shout your e-mail message—write in lowercase.

GEORGE I AM NOT GOING TO ATTEND THAT MEETING

George, I am NOT going to attend that meeting.

George, I am *not* going to attend that meeting.

- **DON'T forget to sign your messages.** You should type a closing comment, then your name or your initials at the end of each message. This both signals your reader you have finished making your comments as well as makes your message friendlier and humanizes the text.
- **DO double-space in between your paragraphs when you can.** The additional space in between paragraphs makes it easier to read on the screen (or even on the printer if your reader decides to print it).
- **DON'T forget to write to your reader.** Think about the audience when you send technical information over e-mail. When in doubt, use a couple of extra words to explain things. For example, if you are corresponding with people who are new to computers, de-

fine your terms promptly using parentheses or dashes. Here are two examples: (1) The modem (for modulator-demodulator) is a device that can be attached to let your computer communicate with other computers over telephone lines. (2) One project goal is to provide a network—a group of interconnected computers—with almost unlimited memory and computational power.

- **DO consider using document compression software.** If you use a commercial e-mail system and want to send large documents, you will find they transmit faster when they are compressed. Commercial products like PKZIP by PKWare lets you take a file, or group of files, and neatly compress them into a smaller size. The document(s) file will be smaller, require less time to send, and take less storage space on the e-mail system. Consequently, your storage and transmission costs will be lower. One caveat: The person on the other end will have to uncompress the document(s) before using them.

- **DO brainstorm with others on your e-mail system.** Sharing ideas can help solve problems for your company or your client. Sharing e-mail messages with a number of people might help invite other opinions to help resolve an issue.

- **DO learn how to send e-mail to a distribution list.** Most e-mail systems have a handy feature for creating distribution lists. By creating several of these lists, you can save time when you want a group of people to get your messages and notes.

- **DON'T forget to use caution when sending personal information.** Even if your company does not have a policy about the privacy of the individual employee's e-mail, your messages and notes may be monitored. So far the legal process has produced consistent results: The courts favor e-mail as a company property, not a personal property.

SETTING UP E-MAIL FOR YOUR COMPANY

If you are lucky (or unlucky) enough to be selected as the person to initiate e-mail in your organization, you have a big job ahead. E-mail selection and implementation is no small task. You will undoubtedly wind up either a hero or a bum.

Making the right decisions will make you a hero. Choosing the right package, making sure it is installed properly, and making sure everyone gets trained and on board will certainly endear you to everyone in the organization. But, one wrong move and you could turn out to be "that idiot who messed up our lives."

In an effort to make you a hero, we offer a few tips. First, we will talk about selecting an e-mail package, then getting one set up and breathing.

Selecting a Marvelous Mail Package

Even though there are many wonderful e-mail packages to choose from, some are more marvelous than others. I

Figure 7.10. There are many great features in today's e-mail packages, but some are greater than others.

like to rate the importance of e-mail features on a scale, 1 to 5, with 1 meaning it is not a very important feature and 5 meaning it is critical. Here is a list of features (and my ratings) you should look for:

Sending Messages

- **CC:** (5) Ability to send courtesy copies.
- **BCC:** (3) Ability to send blind courtesy copies (where receivers do not know the identity of everyone on the copy list).
- **Distribution lists:** (5) Your e-mail system should let you create special lists of people, such as a department or work group. That way, you can address a message to one e-mail address but it will actually send the message to many people.
- **Outgoing log:** (3) Ability to automatically keep a copy of all the messages you send out.
- **Editing features:** (5) At the very least, your e-mail system should let you easily edit your text messages and change them as you need to. Look for how easy it is to cut, copy, and paste messages around the text.
- **Spelling:** (1) Although it is not critical, most people really like a speller for their e-mail. It not only catches the misspelled words, but also the ones you know how to spell but you mistyped.
- **Attachments:** (3) E-mail takes on a more impactful role when you can attach a document to the message. Attachments might be a spreadsheet, a graph, a word-processing document, or a voice or video clip.
- **Reply to:** (1) Some systems let you originate an e-mail on one computer but let you re-direct reply messages to another. This is handy for mobile users who might borrow somebody else's computer to send a message, but want the response back to them.
- **Shared address book:** (3) A shared address book saves everyone time. Instead of everyone having to keep track of the e-mail address of 1500 people, a central list is created and maintained for the organization.
- **Private address book:** (3) A private address book lets you store the e-mail addresses of people that you

need to reach, but are not necessary for everyone else to reach.

- **Insert a file:** (3) It is helpful to be able to bring in another document into your e-mail message.

Receiving Messages

- **In box manipulations:** (5) At the very least, you will want to be able to sort messages in an in box. Different sorts, such as sorting by sender name, date, type of e-mail message, subject, etc., are very helpful.
- **Forwarding:** (5) It is important to have an easy way to forward messages you receive to others. This feature should let you forward to individuals or lists of people.
- **Reply:** (5) Your system should have a one-key (or one-click) feature that automatically lets you reply to messages. This feature should allow you to reply without having to address it back to the sender.
- **Reply-All:** (3) A reply-all feature lets you send your response to the message back to everyone who was on the "To" or "Copy" list. This feature is a real time-saver and helps avoid leaving someone out of the loop when it comes to getting message responses.
- **Folders:** (3) Once you read and act on an e-mail message, you will want to file it some place. It is a real plus if the e-mail package lets you file messages into folders. And, sometimes you might want to file the same message into multiple folders, so look for that feature too.

Tips for Setting Up Your Company's E-mail System

While each system is a little different, most e-mail systems let you have a good bit of freedom in setting up people and functions. We have suggestions to make that should work for almost all e-mail systems. They are:

- **Use a naming scheme.** When you set up people in the e-mail system, use a rational approach toward naming. Do not name people Susie or Joe because you will confuse people and end up with 27 Susies in the organization. Since most e-mail address lists automatically alphabetize names, we suggest you develop a naming scheme that is some combination of the person's name, with the last name coming first. For example:

Name	E-mail ID	E-mail ID
Diane Bolin	Bolin or BolinD	DianeB
Tony Croes	Croes or CroesT	TonyC
Cheryl Currid	Currid or CurridC	CherylC
Dianne Davison	Davison or DavisonD	DianneD
Josh Penrod	Penrod or PenrodJ	JoshP
Paul Penrod	Penrod* or PenrodP	PaulP
Dorothy Wolf	Wolf or WolfD	DorothyD

Table 7.4. Sample naming scheme for setting up the office e-mail.

Even if the e-mail system requires you to use a short name (such as eight characters) you can still make up something intelligible that looks like the person's name.

- **E-mail is for individuals.** Everyone should be a user. Do not ask people to share an e-mail name, such as "Financial Services Department." E-mail works best when everyone has an individual mailbox.

- **No mailboxes for no-users.** Do not set up an e-mail address for people who will not use it. If the president of the company does not have access to e-mail, do not let people make the mistake of sending messages to a dead-letter box.

In some cases, it works to set up an e-mail box for someone when another person will monitor it. Again,

Figure 7.11. Do not send mail to a dead letter box.

if the president of the company does not use e-mail, but his or her secretary does, then it is fine to set up the e-mail address box. The secretary, in effect becomes a switching agent, but the mail gets through.

- **Extra-enterprise e-mail.** Very quickly, e-mail requirements have a way of growing to people outside the immediate organization. You may want to hook up suppliers, agents, contractors, consultants, or even customers. The very best way to arrange for the inevitable growth of e-mail is to find a public service that can act as a third-party mail box. There are a number of companies that will give you an INTERNET address. Or, consider the services of MCI Mail, AT&T EasyLink, or CompuServe for helping route outside mail to your organization.

- **Protect your e-mail.** Make sure your e-mail system is located on a protected computer that gets frequent backups and as much physical security as possible. E-mail quickly becomes a mission-critical application that people rely on. Downtime is not tolerable.

WHAT IS NEXT FOR E-MAIL?

As computer and communications technologies converge, look for e-mail to get a lot more personal. Already, many popular e-mail packages let you include video, audio, and still picture clips. These help you personalize the message.

On the downside, they also make the messages much larger. Large messages can cause problems over slow communications lines, so use caution. It is a good idea to test out audio and video attachments with one or two people before you send 1000 messages with a three-minute video clip of your last trip to Hawaii.

As technology progresses, however, look for more integration of video conferencing and e-mail. Products are coming to market each week that make the technology easy to use. And some of it is fun.

In the next chapter, I am going to introduce another type of e-mail, called groupware. There are subtle but important differences between the two categories of software—so stay tuned.

8

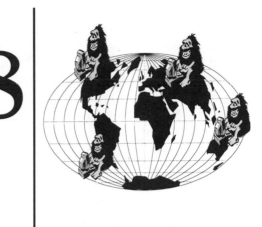

Getting a Grip on Groupware

If you ask five different people to define the term groupware, you will probably get five different answers. To some, it is an extended form of e-mail (or bulletin board) that lets people discuss issues electronically. To others, it helps coordinate work flow by passing information in a special order. To still others, groupware is a data vault or repository where you can collect information. To almost everyone, groupware is a buzz word.

The term "groupware" is one of those magic terms that help products sell. It is almost like using the terms "lite" or "low cal" or "fat free" on foods. So, do not be surprised to see products ranging from group electronic scheduling software to programs that plot your family tree advertise themselves as groupware.

My own definition of groupware is both broad but simple: any application software that supports the information needs of a group. It can be software that routes information, holds it in one place, or lets people tack notes and comments to it. The group part of groupware can be your local team of coworkers, or a group of professionals that spans the globe.

Now, if you are thinking that groupware sounds a lot like e-mail you are on the right track—but there is one big difference. Groupware programs let everybody talk at the same time; e-mail software is based on the premise of one-to-one (or one-after-one) communication. Groupware is more like an electronic bulletin board where people post their information by topic. E-mail is more like a memo or a letter.

Still confused? Read on. This chapter will define the various types of software that make up the software category called groupware. It will also give you an understanding of how groupware may be applied within your organization to boost workgroup productivity.

WHO NEEDS IT?

In today's downsized, employee-empowered, virtualized organizations, you simply cannot manage by the old rules. You need to use any and every electronic trick in the book.

Business executives have trimmed many management layers and flattened hierarchical structures.

It is no longer corporate cool to have one supervisor to every two workers. Do not laugh, I remember the days when consultants would draw organizational charts that looked like narrow pyramids. It was not unusual for companies to have twenty to thirty layers of managers between the president and the line worker.

Figure 8.1. Businesses have trimmed layers of management to make a flattened hierarchical structure.

Delayering or downsizing (the polite terms for cutting out middle management fat) was a popular management practice throughout the late 1980s into the mid-

Figure 8.2. Old style middle management pushed papers and watched the clock.

1990s. It reorganized teams and departments and changed reporting structures so that the worker-to-supervisor ratio grew to ten-to-one. After all, many middle-managers hardly contributed to real work anyway. Old-style middle-managers were clock-watchers, time-keepers, and paper-pushers. Many contributed little more than writing up status reports that took too long to read.

As long ago as 1988, preeminent management guru Peter Drucker warned that middle-managers' role had historically been that of communications. Or, as he put it:

> *"human boosters for the faint, unfocused signals that pass for communications. . ."*
>
> Peter Drucker
> The Coming of the New Organization
> Harvard Business Review
> January/February 1988

Okay, so where does groupware come in? Good groupware is designed to provide communications boosters—electronically. It can cut through organizational boundaries by letting everyone get to key pieces of information easily.

And, it does not matter if the people (group members) work in the same building, work in the same city, or even on the same continent.

In fact, as organizations continue to spread out across the globe, it is very likely that a work group could span several continents. Enter the new wave of office productivity software—groupware.

Figure 8.3. Today, organizations spread across the globe and office productivity survives because of groupware.

The real benefits of using groupware come when people assemble work teams based on talent and not geographic convenience. And they can add up to significant dollars. A 1994 International Data Corporation study of Lotus Notes users revealed that nearly 40 percent saw a payback in less than a year. More than two-thirds saw important business benefits within three years. Further, when asked to account for the financial benefits, the average return on investment was 179 percent. That is pretty impressive.

Properly deployed, the technology lets business managers tap the global gene pool for the best and brightest team members. It lets people get to information and build a body of corporate knowledge.

GROUPWARE MEANS SHARE

Looking back at how people first started connecting with computers, people usually had a single purpose—sharing. They wanted to share printers, share disk storage, and share communications gateways. Groupware takes this fundamental principle of connections to a whole new level. Forget about connecting computers—groupware is all about connecting people.

Now, if you think about it, you begin to see that fundamental components of groupware can be broken down into three basic parts: information sharing; messaging; and collaboration.

Information Sharing

Information sharing is an evolutionary step from today's computer systems and databases. While the underlying principles are basically the same—people put information in the computer and it lets other people see it. But, what is different is the how, what, and why have changed.

In a groupware system, the goal is to improve and build upon team memory. Anybody can put in information, anybody can see it. So, if you believe that broad access to information is critical for a highly efficient work group, then you will buy into the idea of groupware as an information repository or data vault. (The term data vault is only partially accurate. Data vaults in groupware systems are often left unlocked. By virtue of being a group member you get free and open doors to the information.)

The information-sharing component can be important to a workflow design effort. Some tools that can be used to support an information sharing environment are as follows:

- **Workflow design and management systems.** Among the best group productivity tools are workflow systems. These systems are designed to mirror and model procedures like getting a purchase order approved. You can almost classify them as "thing" trackers. A robust workflow design and management system will be flexible enough to let you create a process to manage a help desk, track defects, and then order lunch for the office.

Audits Request

Creates Purchase Request

Approves Request

Pays Invoice

Figure 8.4. Sample of a workflow design and management system.

- **Scheduling.** Have you ever tried to coordinate a meeting among five busy people? It is no small task. Group scheduling systems allow you to check everyone's schedule, resolve conflicts, find a conference room, and recommend the best time and place for the meeting to occur. Sounds simple, but the technology underlying such a system is complex.
- **Document management.** Document management systems allow work groups to place a library of information on line so that anyone can access the information at anytime.

- **Shared databases.** The underlying engine required for sharing bits and pieces of information is a database. But, groupware gives database technology a twist. Most databases require rigidly defined fields, like where to put quantity or unit price. A groupware database usually includes free-form text fields or places to put notes of any size or content. This goes well beyond traditional database architectures. Further, the groupware engine must be smart enough to support and manipulate more than alphanumeric data. People want to store and share images, graphics, voice, video, and about anything else we can think of that has an information content to the database. The trick is consolidating the various pieces back into one logical piece of information.

Messaging

In today's office environment, messaging occurs in a variety of media: voice mail, Post-It™ Notes, fax, electronic mail, and paper memos. Up until recently, e-mail had become the basic foundation passing information to work group members.

But, because of the way e-mail is built, centering on one-to-one communication, it really does not solve the group problem. It does not let people easily track and record comments on a topic-by-topic basis.

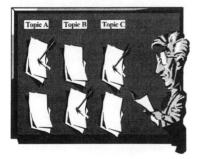

Figure 8.5. Groupware software is similar to a bulletin board.

Using groupware software, people often configure it to start a topic then thread the messages relating to that topic. You can think of it as an electronic bulletin board, arranged by subject. Anybody in the group can pose a question, make a remark, or argue a point. The rule is: Stay on the topic.

Collaboration

The last and least understood component of groupware system is collaboration. This one is the hardest to define, but I am going to give it a try.

Collaboration tools help groups think and work together regardless if they are in the same room or several thousand miles away. Collaboration tools come in a variety of shapes and sizes all designed to facilitate various forms of human interaction. A few examples of collaboration tools are as follows:

- **Brainstorming.** Brainstorming software allows participants to collectively brainstorm various aspects of

Figure 8.6. Collective brainstorming.

  a given project or idea. Software from companies like Vantana allow for electronic meetings in real time. Some groups use products like Lotus Notes for making comments on a topic when all the participants cannot be together at once.

- **Idea organizers.** Idea organization software takes the results of the brainstorming session and condenses the ideas into a set of relevant topics. Any software that automates an outline can be used for this.

- **Group editor.** Group editors allow individuals to contribute sections to a working document while commenting on other people's work without affecting their original inputs. Some people use special software for this while others simply turn on the revision feature of a word processing package, like Microsoft Word.

- **Video conferencing.** Video conferencing systems provide a mechanism that supports real-time transmission of voice and video signals. Today's systems can be either conference-room- or desktop-oriented. Recent advances in desktop video teleconferencing technology will begin to fill a void of personal communications on an ad hoc basis. In addition, desktop video teleconferencing systems will also support non-real time communications in the form of electronic video notes and files. Chapter 10 discusses these systems in detail.

TIPS ON SETTING UP AND USING GROUPWARE

Since groupware is so many things to so many people, it is hard to give very specific tips. Fear not, I have still prepared a list for you. Keep in mind that these tips cover all kinds of groupware applications so not all of them might apply to you. Here goes:

- **Mind your manners—don't change the subject.** It is both uncool and uncouth to leave off-topic messages

Figure 8.7. Show good manners when you are working in groupware.

in a groupware forum. If you are using a groupware application for group messaging about the new widget development project, be careful to stay on task, on topic, and focused. Do not leave any messages about how you went sailing with Aunt Martha last week or that you are going to sell your old car. Nobody appreciates junk mail, junk e-mail, or junk groupware messages.

- **Use the right tool for the message.** Remember, the difference between groupware and e-mail is a matter of topic and audience. If you have a message to send about the topic, use groupware. If you want to send a private note to Fred, use e-mail.

- **Watch out for workflow.** One of modern software's greatest innovations has been workflow. With it you can route around approval forms, expense requests, and other types of electronic documents. Now, before you go charging off to redevelop all your work processes, take a look at the steps you automate. If you have a thirty-one person sign-off for a capital expense request, perhaps you should consider reducing the number of signatures. Sure, you can automate the process and make it go faster, but you will not get the real benefit of the software. You will only speed up the mess.

- **Free up your form.** Do not become a prisoner of old-style paper forms. If you are about to recreate your company's forms with software, consider revising the style and content. And, remember, screens have fewer lines than paper, so try to get most of the important and related information in screen size input forms.

- **Use group scheduling for meetings.** I am always amazed to see organizations that have scheduling software, but do not use it. Instead, executives and managers send their assistants off to hours and hours of telephone tag trying to schedule meetings.

Figure 8.8. Use scheduling software rather than searching through calendars for compatible appointment times.

George is open Wednesday; but Fred is going to be out of town; and Lori is pre-paring for a board meeting. Rather than ask humans to unsnarl complex schedules, get the computer to do it. Most scheduling software, like Novell's GroupWise, can search schedules and come up with several options. Then, the software can invite participants. This stuff really works!

- **Build your bases.** One of the most valuable assets is what is inside peoples' heads—knowledge. You can use groupware to build up those knowledge bases by storing documents by topic. Products like Lotus Notes can easily be set up as a knowledge base.

- **If it moves, automate it!** Look through your existing manual paper-passing processes. Does that process add any value? If it does, then find a way to give it electronic wings. Products like Delrina's FormFlow or Action Technologies WorkFlow software can easily move work from place to place. Remember: If something moves from one desk to another, you can automate it.

THE DARK SIDE OF GROUPWARE

Despite my raving and ranting accolades to the goodness of groupware, there are several potholes on the way to

Figure 8.9. There are many potholes on the way to paradise.

paradise. While the technology is improved greatly over the past few years, groupware takes a lot of preplanning. My general words of wisdom—tread lightly and remain flexible.

In my research and consulting practice, I see three areas where organizations slip and trip up their installations. They are: inadequate infrastructure, poor technology selections, and creepy corporate cultures. Let me explain:

Inadequate Infrastructure

If your organization is still limping along with a computer network designed to share printers or disk space, you could be in big trouble. Most groupware packages assume that you have fixed all the glitches in your network design so that it is capable of running an active shared database.

If you are not sure how stable or well-built your network is, then call in a consultant. A quick look does not cost much and could save you a lot of grief. After all,

Figure 8.10. Make sure you have a solid foundation for your infrastructure.

most people would not think of adding a major addition to their homes without consulting with a structural engineer. The same logic should apply to your groupware installation. Network dynamics will change, storage requirements will change, and traffic patterns will be altered. An inadequate infrastructure could be your doom before you even begin. It is important to note that you must consider both the LAN architecture and the computing environment.

Poor Technology Selections

Beware—not all software packages work well together. Moreover not all software runs on all computers. If your company has both Macs and standard PCs, then your

Figure 8.11. Remember, not everything works with everything else.

software needs to support both platforms. Otherwise somebody (likely the person with the Mac) will not be able to join the group with groupware.

Other pitfalls come from selecting the wrong tool for the job. Remember, just because Lotus Notes "can" be programmed to do just about anything, it does not mean it "should." When you are selecting the technology for your groupware package, make sure you survey the market carefully. Sometimes a specific package will cost you more to buy, but save you hours, headaches, and heartaches later on.

The computer industry has a habit sometimes of promoting several conflicting standards. It is important to understand the consequences of each product.

Creepy Corporate Cultures

Success with groupware can largely depend on your corporate culture. If your culture is win-win, we are all in

Figure 8.12. Sharing knowledge is vital for a win-win environment when using groupware.

this for the good of the company—then groupware will enhance your ability to share knowledge. Conversely, if your organization is full of people who are trying to look good at someone else's expense, then you are in for a challenge. People who hoard information and use it as power will not cotton to giving up their hard won knowledge to a groupware package.

Now, for some good news. Organizational dynamics can change once people get used to using groupware technology. I can recall two consulting firms who were early adopters of Lotus Notes. In the first case, the consultants went wildly populating the knowledge base with great information. The firm saw an almost instant boost in its ability to solve clients problems. The second firm struggled for nearly two years, begging its consultants to contribute their knowledge. In this case, the ingrained culture said: "knowledge is power and promotions, I am not going to share it." Over time, and a lot of cajoling from senior partners, the culture changed. Ultimately, the consultants did start sharing their knowledge and their business has since strengthened.

The questions you have to ask are: Can you and your colleagues adapt? Will your firm's managers become cheerleaders for change? Are you willing to change processes if you need to? If your answers are "no," then you are better off spending your time, effort, and money on another technology.

THE FUTURE: WHERE IS GROUPWARE GOING?

Groupware is targeted at the most precious resources in today's fast moving organization—time and knowledge. As you begin to use it, it will allow your organization to reduce overall cycle time, improve decisions, and empower knowledge teams at all levels.

Over the past few years, the technology itself has matured to the point where it has become highly refined and sophisticated. IBM's Lotus Notes product has become standard issue among knowledge-based companies, like consultants, law firms, and service organizations. New products such as the Microsoft Exchange and Novell's GroupWise will develop and raise the standards of sophistication.

Look for the category of groupware products to merge with other collaborative tools. Desktop video conferences, for example, could be stored and indexed by groupware software. Then, if you only want to review part of the last status meeting, say Joe's comments about the competition in the super-size widget category, you could select just that portion.

Moreover, groupware is likely to cause people to expand their focus beyond the body of knowledge currently held by the company. Look for organizations to reach out, perhaps into cyberspace, to increase the size and the quality of group and the base of knowledge. And, speaking of cyberspace, stay tuned for the next chapter.

9

The Great Race to Cyberspace

Sooner or later nearly everyone who survives the learning curve of computers and communications is going to want to branch out—go beyond the PC, beyond the LAN, and beyond the office e-mail system. Curious people want to take that extra step and see what is on the other side of a modem.

For those who do venture out, there is good news. Planet Earth is filled with fascinating information resources. There are public services that let you send e-mail to almost anyone. Then, there are special interest forums on services like CompuServe, America Online, or Prodigy that can turn into electronic town meetings of people wanting to share information.

Sound good? Sure, but for business people expecting to stay on top of their field, cyberspace is more than just a place to satisfy intellectual curiosity. In fact, already for some, it is necessary to make a daily trek somewhere into the Internet or commercial online services to research facts or look for news. With information becoming readily available, there is just no excuse for "not knowing."

Does this mean there is a gold rush for online services? If it has not already started in your industry, rest assured that it will. And, you should be learning all you can about what is available from the world of on-line services for your business or industry. If you do not, your competitor will.

Figure 9.1. Remember, your competitor is not standing behind you but trying to pass you at your expense.

When you first fire up your modem and get to cyberspace, you will have plenty of company. Online services, such as CompuServe and America Online, each have better than three million subscribers. Prodigy boasts nearly two million and counts over 22,000 messages daily in the art club alone. Then, of course, there is galactic central, the Internet, with more than 30 million users worldwide.

You can meet people electronically and share information, news and views with your electronic friends. While many business people might at first shrug off the notion of spending time chatting online, this social aspect of computing turns out to be a favorite pastime. It is like going to an electronic global gab fest. By using the Internet, or online services, you are not limited to reading the views of people in your local area. Your fellow participants are as likely to come from remote places around the globe as the house down the street.

Now, back to business. You name it, you can find it. Are you looking for an article written three years ago on derivatives? Would you like to see the latest earnings report on your competitor? How about checking today's weather forecast in Bolivia? You can find it online, and if you know where to look, you can find it in a flash!

Many business and trade magazines make the full text of articles available through powerful search engines. For example, CMP, a leading publisher of computer trade magazines, put the entire text of its eleven publications on the Internet in a searchable database called TechWeb. To use the system, you simply need to type in a few key words and whoosh, you will get back the titles of articles written within the last year. Then, to see the full text, you need only select from the list on your screen.

But, another caution comes here, these services can be habit-forming. I know of people who are "knowledge junkies" spending lots of time looking up anything their hearts (or brains) desire. (Admittedly, I am one myself.)

Fasten Your Seatbelts!

This chapter takes you on a tour of the great public and commercial on-line e-mail and database services, which is sometimes called cyberspace. Even if you are a total newbie (newcomer) just starting out, it should help you feel comfortable to start your modem.

First, I will give you a quick road map to the Internet—the global web of interconnected computers that is chock-full of information, knowledge, and entertainment. I will not provide details of every nook and cranny, but I will give you a top-line view of where you need to point your attention.

Then I will give you a glimpse at the offerings from some of the more popular commercial services, such as CompuServe, America Online, Prodigy, and the Microsoft Network. These services are worth their monthly fees because they organize information for you.

I will also cover the basics of electronic etiquette—netiquette—so you will know how to behave and how to avoid looking like a digital dummy.

CURRID'S QUICK AND DIRTY TRAVEL GUIDE TO THE INTERNET

You do not need a license to navigate the Internet, but it

is a good idea to learn the rules of the road before you rev up your modem and race on. It takes a little learning before you get the keys to unlock the greatest collection of knowledge on planet Earth.

Figure 9.2. Know the rules of the road.

What is the Internet?

The Internet is a collection of computers that are hooked up to over 45 thousand networks worldwide. While analysts believe there are over 30 million Internet users, there could be a lot more if you consider the people who connect to other networks that pass information to the Internet. These other networks can be as small as a private bulletin board system (BBS) that serves only a few people a day, up to a government network that connects thousands. And, before the decade is over, analysts expect that Internet growth will surely triple.

In the early 1980s, there were only 200 host computers on Internet. By 1991, there were more than 300,000, and by mid-1994, analysts estimate 3.2 million host computers were connected to the "Net."

Fueling this frenetic growth is good old fashion capitalism. The commercial domain, meaning your business and mine, continues to multiply growing by 30 percent or more a quarter. As of late 1994, there were over one million commercial hosts.

Today, on the Internet, you can look up photographs of new automobiles, houses for sale, and informa-

Figure 9.3. You can dream on the Internet about new houses and sports cars.

tion about myriads of other consumer products. More importantly for business, you can reach into the research of universities worldwide. And, you can find a direct link to just about any large company who freely publishes product information. That is the good news.

The bad news is that it is not always so easy to find your way around the Net. Using the Internet for business is like going to a giant library—without a card file system. You could spend hours or days fixated at your computer's screen roaming around the global web.

The Internet was not designed to serve the common person. It was originally built in the late 1960s by grants from the U.S. Department of Defense as a place that scientists and researchers working for the government could share information. They wanted to make sure that nothing, including a thermonuclear war, could ever stop the flow of information. As a result, they invented a special protocol for packet switching and called it TCP/IP (Transmission Control Protocol/Internet Protocol). This protocol is still in use today.

Up until the mid-1980s use of the Internet was strictly limited to government and university sites.

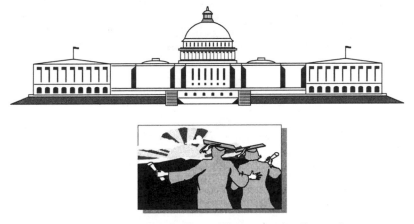

Figure 9.4. Government and universities were the first to have access to the Internet.

The Internet was built as a network of interconnected computers that could not be destroyed. It has no beginning or no end. By design, if a computer link goes down, others will route messages around it.

Also, the Internet has no built-in security. Because it was built for sharing information, its creators did not wish to put in arbitrary measures that would keep people out. (That design feature has proved to be both a blessing and a curse.)

Today, companies like Netscape and others have built software that allows people to complete secure transactions over the Internet. This opens up the way for credit card purchases and other business transactions. Beware, however, because for every security program, there are thousands of hackers trying to break it. Netscape's security posed such a challenge that a student enrolled at Ecole Polytechnique in France lined up a network of 120 workstation computers and a supercomputer to break part of the code.

Figure 9.5. Beware of security. There are hackers trying to break in to the system.

What You Need to Know About the Net

If you are just getting started or brand new to the Internet, there are a few things you should know. First you will need the proper equipment in your office (or home or both). This means a computer, a communicating device, a logon ID or address, software, and probably a printer. Then, once you have set up your computer, you need to know how to aim your search.

The Communicating Device

Your communicating device can be a modem (preferably a fast one, that can support 28,800 bps speed) or an ISDN connection. If you do not have a clue about setting up this equipment, head straight to your favorite computer store, consultant, or corporate information support team.

Keep in mind, your access to the Internet will only go as fast as the slowest link. For example, if you work for ABC Big Company, who has a 128KB line into the Internet, but you dial in to it from your home with your 14,000 bps modem, your transmission will never go faster than the modem. And, sadly, it will probably go a lot slower depending on the software you use to get from your home to your office network to the Internet. So remember, everything you do counts.

Addresses in Cyberspace

Next you need to get a logon ID or a cyberspace e-mail address. This is a name that you receive from your Internet provider or your employer. You may be using a national or regional provider, such as Netcom, or Houston-based NeoSoft, or a commercial service. Providers open up an account in your name and give you a phone number to call, or a link to their high-speed lines. Alternatively, if you are a member of a commercial service, like CompuServe, America Online, Prodigy, or the Microsoft Network, you already have Internet access. You can get to most of the Internet directly from these services.

Just like a postal address, your cyberspace address will follow a convention. The scheme consists of a name to identify you and one to identify the domain. The common format is to place the user name first, an *at* sign (@), then the domain name, such as:

myname@myplace.com

The domain, after the @ sign, tells you the name of the organization that runs a site, what kind of site it is, and what country it is in. Large organizations may have more than one computer tied to the Internet, so you could see a two-part domain name. Sometimes you will even run across three- or four-part domain names, such as:

joes@bigco.nyc.west.com

which could stand for Joe Smith at Big Company, in New York City, West building, a commercial site.

Generally, a basic net address looks simple, something like this:

currid@radiomail.net

Here, currid is the individual user's ID. This individual can be found at a site, or domain, known as radiomail.net.

If you are working on designing your own company's setup, make sure you scream, holler, and raise the roof over the company's naming convention. If your company decides to name you r2d2@bigco.com, only your work colleagues (with a cheat sheet), and maybe your closest friends will know who you are.

Addresses for Locations

While I am talking about addresses, keep in mind that organizations have addresses too. These are called URLs (pronounced earls), which stands for uniform resource locator. If your company has registered itself with the InterNIC on the Internet's World Wide Web (WWW), it has probably taken an address (or URL) that can be accessed easily from any Internet browser software. For example, some popular computer and communications companies have set themselves up as:

Company	Internet WWW Address
Advanced Micro Devices	http://www.amd.com
Ameritech	http://www.ameritech.com
AT&T	http://www.att.com
Compaq Computer Corp.	http://www.compaq. com
Hewlett-Packard	http://www.hp.com
IBM	http://www.ibm.com
Intel	http://www.intel.com
Microsoft	http://www.microsoft.com
Novell	http://www.novell.com

Table 9.1. Some popular Internet company addresses.

See the trend? It is not too difficult to guess the addresses of large companies. Unfortunately, this easy naming standard is not universal. If you guess the name and cannot locate the company, it may be listed under a different name or a longer name. You can check with one of the many Internet directory services (mentioned later) or call the company to get its official Internet address.

Also, the last part of an Internet address usually follows a convention. Within the United States, Internet addresses usually end in an organizational suffix, such as .com for a commercial business, .edu for a college, university, or other educational institution, or .org for an organization. Other U.S. based suffixes include:

.gov for government

.mil for military agencies

.net for organizations that run large networks

Sites outside the United States commonly use a two-letter code to represent the country such as: .au for Australia; .ca for Canada; .fr for France; or .ch for Switzerland. (Okay, they don't all make sense.)

Types of Services

The top services on the Internet give you access to e-mail, WWW, discussion or news groups, and more. You can also transfer files using FTP (File Transfer Protocol), which is a protocol that lets you exchange files with an Internet host computer. Moreover, there are powerful search engines that let you look up addresses of sites that might store information you want to see. You might not need to use all the services available, but here is a quick list to describe the popular tools and services:

- **E-mail:** When you get your Internet account, you will likely get an Internet e-mail address with it. Some Internet providers distribute a shareware version of a program called Eudora Mail by Qualcomm. If you use Microsoft Mail, Novell's GroupWise, or IBM Lotus cc:Mail, or other popular packages, your company's e-mail administrator may be able to hook up your company's e-mail system directly. Such a direct link will allow Internet transported messages to show up in your in box. If you have an account with a commercial service like CompuServe or America Online, you can direct your Internet mail to that address. Otherwise, there are a host of low-cost (or no-cost) software packages to let you manage your Internet e-mail.

- **Finger:** If you know another person's Internet address, you can "finger" them to see if they are currently logged on. If you are using a WWW (World Wide Web) browser, you can check by going over to: http://www.winternet.com/~drow/finger.html.
- **FTP (File Transfer Protocol):** You can transfer files between computers on the Internet using a software standard called FTP. Many organizations and universities offer FTP sites so people can easily exchange files.
- **Gopher and Veronica:** Because the Internet is so vast (and relatively undocumented) people have built search engines called Gophers. These are tools that let you locate and browse resources from a series of lists. But, now that there are so many Gopher sites, another tool, Veronica, has been developed to help you find the Gopher servers.
- **IRC (Internet Relay Chat):** This feature lets people carry on a real-time conversation back and forth over the Internet.
- **Listservs:** Many organizations offer broadcast services to keep people informed of events or updates on a topic. These are called LISTSERV services. Generally you can join (or "subscribe") by sending a message to the listserver who will add your e-mail address to the list. Then, whenever something is posted to the listserver, everyone automatically gets the message. If you get flooded with unwanted messages, you can al-

ways "unsubscribe" or suspend your e-mail address to cut off the barrage of mail.

- **USENET newsgroups:** Name your subject, from news about aeronautical engineering to discussions on zebra fish research—you can find somebody saying something on a USENET (user network) newsgroup. These freeform discussions allow everybody to contribute "articles" or messages on a topic. Often, people post questions, like "where can I find?" or, "anybody know what car I should buy?"

  Newsgroups can be moderated or unmoderated. With moderated groups, you send your message to the moderator who determines whether it is worthy of posting for all to see. The moderator acts as a filter and generally keeps the newsgroup messages focused on a topic. Unmoderated newsgroups provide a forum for free speech. Virtually anybody with a keyboard can spill out news and views.

  Despite the relatively chaotic appearance of newsgroups, they are arranged by broad topic levels. There are seven top-level categories:

Top-Level Category	Issues
comp	Computer subjects
misc	Topics not covered by other categories
news	Network, newsgroup, and administrative information
rec	Recreational topics
sci	Physical and social science subjects
soc	Social and cultural topics
alt*	Alternative topics (not technically a part of usenet newsgroups, but often very popular)

Table 9.2. Example of seven top-level newsgroups.

- **WAIS (Wide Area Information Server):** This is special server software that lets people store documents in a database. Users can quickly search for articles or other text based on key word searches. For example, if you want to search all the articles written about Windows 95 in the news magazine *Information Week*, you can locate them through a WAIS search.
- **WWW (World Wide Web):** This is the place you will likely spend most of your time. It is a collection of computers around the globe that lets you read information posted in hypertext. The WWW requires that you use special "browser" software, like Netscape or the browser software available from your commercial on-line service. This software interprets the hypertext links and language called HTML (which stands for hypertext markup language).

You can also move from place to place by following hypertext linked files. For example, if you are reading

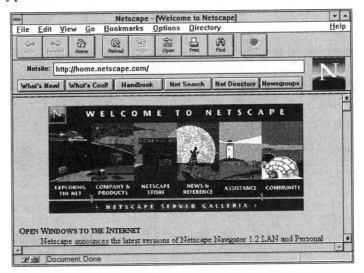

Figure 9.6. NetScape WWW browser.

about a special piece of information and there is a hypertext reference to another site, you need only to point to the reference and click on your mouse button. Whoosh, instantly you are transported to that location. Then, if you want to go back, you simply use the "back" button on your browser to return to your original location.

Search Services

Despite the wealth of knowledge available on the Internet, many people complain that it is still too hard to find what they want. Enter the super-searchers. Services like Lycos, Yahoo, and Webcrawler index the contents of thousands of other sites. If you do not know where to start looking about a subject, first try one of the Internet addresses shown in Table 9.3. They will help point you in the right direction.

Service	Internet Address
Lycos	http://lycos.cs.cmu.edu/
Webcrawler	http://webcrawler.com/
Einet	http://www.einet.net/
Aliweb	http://web.nexor.co.uk/public/aliweb/search/doc/form.html
CUSI Search	http://pubweb.nexor.co.uk/public/cusi/cusi.html
Yahoo	http://search.yahoo.com/

Table 9.3. List of super searchers for the Internet.

COMMERCIAL INFORMATION SERVICES

If you are looking for a little more consistency and content in your cyber-life, then check out some of the commercial services. For about 10 million of cyber-voyagers, services like CompuServe, America Online, and Prodigy are home base.

All commercial computing services are a little different. They sometimes price services by the service, connection time, or other factor. Many of them have low entry costs, such as $7.95 per month for limited services. But, beware—those costs escalate rapidly if you venture into certain parts of the systems. Make sure you know exactly where you are going or a $7.95 bill might run up to $500 without your knowing it.

The market for commercial services is evolving. There used to be clear lines of difference and these services catered to one of three interest areas: e-mail messaging, research, or electronic forums. As the services have grown and matured over the years, and with competition from the Internet, there is now a lot of blur when it comes to drawing definite lines or trying to neatly categorize them into boxes.

For my purposes here, I will highlight some of the more popular services that provide general interest topics and research.

General Purpose/Forum Focused Services

Some online computer services offer a wide variety of information products. You can find everything from the latest news, weather forecasts, encyclopedia, shopping services, travel, and hobby information. One such service

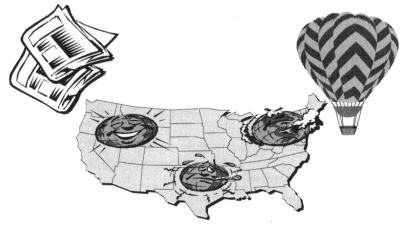

Figure 9.7. Online services offer news stories, weather forecasts, and travel information.

is CompuServe, which boasts access to over 1500 online databases. From looking up the text of last week's *Fortune* Magazine to finding a five-year-old article from the *Harvard Business Review*, CompuServe has a link to just about everything. And, with their forums (like the Internet's newsgroups) you can chat back and forth with other users who have a particular interest in any area from aerobics to zoology.

Along with CompuServe, America Online, Prodigy, and the Microsoft Network also offer many similar services. All offer news, chat forums, e-mail, and periodic special interest events. While these services have yet to replace the daily newspaper as a person's primary information source, you can use them to dig into a lot of information and get results back very quickly.

In recent years, online services have added entertainment to the list of features and services. Want to dial up and participate in an interactive chat with your favorite rock star? Check the listings, but chances are you will find this activity on one of the online services.

Why use it?

General purpose online services are a boon to individuals and organizations alike. They provide a quick and handy

Figure 9.8. Online services may someday replace libraries and access to hard cover printed books.

way to go get specific information. I believe these services will someday replace (or at least greatly supplement) libraries and printed newspapers.

Most users, however, use these services for their social activities. These services all contain electronic forums where people meet and congregate about a particular topic. It could be amateur photography, art collecting, wine tasting, or personal computers. An interesting byproduct of these forums is the evolving social interaction that takes place. People have developed great online dialogs, friendships, and emotional attachments with others that they have only met online.

Overall, these services can be great time-savers. Some even allow for custom clipping of news to create your own news service of just stories pertaining to your particular interests. For example, among the activities at

Figure 9.9. Many services offer custom clipping of news to create your own news service.

Currid & Company, we research specific technology events. Rather than comb newspapers and press clippings for our research, we have set up a CompuServe clippings file in the Executive News Service area. This clipping file lets us specify newspapers and periodicals to search and key words that appear in stories. Whenever a story passes by that contains our search words, it is automatically clipped and placed in an electronic folder for us. This service is a much more accurate reader than a human so it is unlikely that any story ever gets missed.

Of course, there are many other features available through these online services. They will have a specific meaning and value to you depending on your individual situation.

Caveats

Online information services, unlike the Internet, are not free. While many of them offer a low-cost subscription fee, the really good services usually come at an incremental cost. Be sure you know what you are doing when you access these services. If you pull a special research report, make sure you know how much it costs.

Also, some people experience difficulty dealing with the electronic community. This shows up with electronic forums. See the tips throughout this chapter about how to behave on forums.

Examples of Online Services

Listed below are some of the online services available for the public to use.

- **CompuServe:** Among the oldest, largest, and best known public computing services is CompuServe. Founded in 1969, CompuServe has become a popular meeting ground for people in the computer industry. Some people call it an online city—because it has so many places to go and visit. Many of the hardware and software companies have opened up electronic forums so users can congregate and get support.

   CompuServe offers just about every service you could expect from on-line computing. It offers its own e-mail where members can communicate with other

CompuServe users, or the outside world via the Internet; electronic forums; news; stock quotes; electronic encyclopedias; travel information; weather; shopping services; and a host of other services. You can even get to a view of broadcast news through CompuServe's innovative link with CNN online.

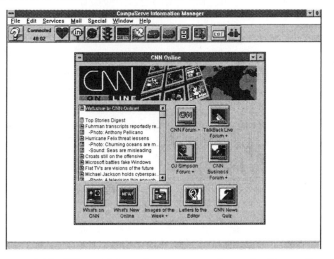

Figure 9.10. View of broadcast news through CompuServe's CNN online link.

You can access CompuServe with regular communications software or specially written software. If you use regular communications software, such as Procomm, you will find the CompuServe menus, prompts, and screens a little old-fashioned. You will probably need to get some training to maneuver around the system and find its many services. If you use the CompuServe software, your life will be a lot easier. This software, called CIM (for CompuServe Information Manager) or WINCIM for (Windows CompuServe Information Manager), creates an attractive interface on your PC and lets you easily interact with all the services available. WINCIM, released in early 1993, brought a new level of easy-to-use software to the market.

- **Prodigy:** Prodigy is a fine, well-rounded service for home users and some business users too. It comes with special software that accesses the system and displays all options with a series of menus and prompts.

  Prodigy does a good job supporting forums for hobbies and entertainment. There are more than 400 special interest groups represented in its forums. And, like CompuServe, Prodigy offers an e-mail facility that exists within Prodigy that logs over 90,000 new messages a day. With special software, Prodigy's e-mail can be accessed off-line.

- **America Online (AOL):** Like CompuServe, America Online attempts to attract business and professional users with a wide offering of current news. Among the news connections it offers are *BusinessWeek*, *Time*, and a host of other business and technical magazines. AOL is best known for its interactive chat lines. They maintain a number of chat rooms where people from 6 to 60 can logon and type real-time messages back and forth. America Online does the best job of policing its cyber-chat rooms and will cancel the service of anyone who uses undesirable words or behavior. (Watch your kids! AOL is serious about keeping a wholesome atmosphere.)

- **Microsoft Network:** The newest of the online networks, MSN was launched with Windows 95 in August of 1995. It is available only to people who use Windows 95. MSN promises to redefine online services, not necessarily with new content—right now it carries about the same information that other services provide—but with ease of access. Getting to MSN is a smooth process with one-button access from your desk.

Research Focused

Some services do not necessarily try to be all things to all people. Instead, these services allow you to interact with computer databases. These databases store silos of books, articles, magazines, and old newspapers.

If you have never used online research you are in for two things: a trick and a treat. The *trick* is the bill that adds up so fast you will not believe your eyes. It is easy to rack up $100–300 in a short search of your favor-

Figure 9.11. Research services will give you both a trick and a treat. The trick is an expensive bill, but the treat comes with pinpoint and fast access to valuable information.

ite topic. The *treat* is finding a great reservoir of information at your fingertips. Once you learn how to use these services, you will never again want to go back to the library and research something the old fashion way.

Why Use Electronic Research Services?

Research services can save you a lot of time and effort combing through books and periodicals. In our information-dependent society, they can help you gain a better perspective on your business and make more informed decisions.

If you know where to look, you can look up almost anything online from such listings of Who's Who in a certain industry, to the encyclopedia explanation of rocket technology.

Caveats

Research services are expensive and sometimes hard to use. Also, you should learn as much as you can about efficient searching techniques for the services you use. Most online research services let you pinpoint your searches with some kind of Boolean logic—the problem is, few of us know how to best apply the search criteria.

Listed below are some research services available today.

- **Dialog:** Dialog is a focused research service with many databases covering books and periodicals in print. It contains the widest variety of databases available. It also provides a number of database combinations that let you search multiple sources at one time. Dialog is not cheap—depending on what service you are using, you can easily run up a bill of several hundred dollars—but it does contain vast amounts of data from a very wide variety of sources.
- **First!** This service is an electronic clippings service that uses a different model. You do not call it, it calls you. It sends e-mail or faxes directly to you, rather than you calling it. You set up your search criteria (industry, periodicals, topics, keywords, etc.) and the electronic robot reads thousands of articles nightly. When it finds an article that meets your search criteria, it puts it in your mailbox.
- **Lexis-Nexis:** These services, formerly Mead Data Central, are a division of Reed International PLC and Elsevier NV. Nexis covers news and Lexis is targeted at the legal profession. The service features ad hoc re-

trievals and has been experimenting with speech recognition programs so that professionals, like lawyers, can call in their search queries.

- **Dow Jones News/Retrieval:** The Dow Jones News/ Retrieval Service (DJNS) is aimed at providing information to investors. It contains current and historical stock prices, bond information, and a variety of news stories from major business publications, such as the *Wall Street Journal*, and *BusinessWeek*.

NETIQUETTE: HOW TO BEHAVE IN ELECTRONIC PUBLIC

As you venture out into public electronic forums, make sure you mind your manners. Cyberspace is certainly a friendly place, but there is little tolerance for people who do not know how to act. You will find there are wonderful friendships to be made with your new electronic community—but you will also find a different style of communication is also needed.

DOs and DON'Ts of Netiquette for Newsgroups and Online Forums

- **DO use your real name.** Phony names and handles do not cut it in the electronic age. Make sure you use your real name when you sign on to public forums.
- **DON'T post phone numbers.** It is not a good idea to leave your private telephone numbers on a public forum. You never know who might be lurking around and could use your number to call to bug you every morning at 3:00 A.M.
- **DO watch what you say in public.** If you are spending time on an Internet discussion group or any kind of interactive chat, watch your language. Some discussions are best taken off-line and settled by private mail. If you are about to launch into a heated discussion with an individual about anything, it might be a

good idea to settle it with him or her by private e-mail and not a public forum. Remember, anyone can read and capture your comments on forums.

- **DO beware of flame-mail.** Flaming on an online service is worse than flaming over regular e-mail. You are likely to embarrass yourself in front of many more people than just one.

- **DO keep messages short.** Try to keep your messages down to one or two paragraphs, if possible. If your message must contain more, then summarize the points in the first or second paragraph.

- **DO limit line length.** Your forum messages will be read by people with a host of different computing devices. Since you do not know how the lines will wrap around their viewing screen, try to keep the line length short—under fifty or sixty characters per line.

- **DO be careful about how you respond to forum messages.** It is very easy to get side-tracked and hit a few keys too hard. E-mailer's remorse can set in very quickly if you fire off a sarcastic message to an electronic forum. Generally speaking, there is no way to get your message back once you have sent it. Remember my cautions about flaming from Chapter 7. Take a deep breath, walk around your computer, or shut it off for a while. Do not send back a flaming message unless you are very willing to deal with the consequences.

- **DON'T forget about the company that keeps you.** If you use a company account to post messages to news groups or forums, be especially careful. Keep personal opinions to yourself. Imagine the public embarrassment of someone named JohnDoe@IBM.COM if he starts flaming over a technical issue on a Compaq Computer. Even if John is speaking his own mind, his e-mail ID makes it look like he speaks for the company. So, if you have something to say that could negatively impact your company, either do not say it or log off, then log back on using a personal account, like JohnDoe@Prodigy.COM.

- **DON'T be a lurker forever.** People who read electronic forum messages, but never contribute any comments are called lurkers. While it is acceptable to be a lurker for a while, your presence on the forum will not add value until you get involved. Find a forum that interests you, then look for a chance to share your opinion or ask a question. You may be pleasantly surprised at how easy it is to interact with electronic friends. On the other hand, do not waste everyone's time sending "un huh" messages.

- **DO stay on topic.** Newsgroups, like forums on CompuServe and America Online, are organized by topic. Do not post a message asking if others believe in gun control in the middle of a forum discussing tropical plants. It does not fit and your fellow users will not be appreciative or amused.

- **DO stick to one topic per message.** If you have several things to say, then send several messages. Most readers will scan the subject line to figure out if they want to read the whole message. They do not like messages to wander from topic to topic.

- **DON'T "spam."** Spamming is the practice of posting the same query to several newsgroups. Many people with similar interests read the same groups and do not appreciate reading a posting several times.

- **DON'T post a specific question to a discussion group; ask for replies by e-mail.** If you have something that is very specific and probably not of interest to the general group, do not inflict others with potentially hundreds of uninteresting messages. Ask that people reply via e-mail, directly to you rather than posting their responses for all the group to see.

- **DON'T use a shared account with listservs.** You may be fascinated by the propagation habits of bromeliads, but do not inflict your work colleagues with 300 message a week on the topic. If your Internet e-mail account is shared with other people, do not subscribe to a listserver with it.

- **DO take a vacation from listservs.** If you are going away for more than a few days, unsubscribe or suspend mail from any mailing lists or LISTSERV services. Otherwise, you will likely find more messages than you can handle upon your return. Also, consider your disk space. While a few messages will not take up much room, you could gobble up lots of space if you have 300 incoming messages.

- **DO set up filters, rules, and folders.** If you are on a listserv mailing list, then be careful to maintain your in box. Active lists can pump out hundreds of messages your way. Dealing with them is like trying to take a sip out of an e-mail fire hose. Check out your e-mail system to see if it can filter the incoming messages. For example, Novell's GroupWise lets users set up rules and will automatically file certain messages in a special folder. You can set up a rule that files all messages with the words "smtp information" in a folder. That way, the system (not you) will file the messages in an appropriate place.

How to Avoid Being Branded a Digital Dummy

When you first begin using public information services, you will most likely feel like a digital dummy. Most of the services are easy to use, but not necessarily easy to learn. They all have their own set of commands, shortcuts, user-to-user lingo, and special quirks.

If you are brand new to cyberspace, try out one of the commercial services first. These services are more orderly for online researching. You will spend less time in infinite loops looking up things that just might not be available.

Experience is the best teacher for online services. The more time you spend online with them, the more comfortable you will become. Even though these services are all a little different, your knowledge is transferable from one to another. If you become an ace researcher on the forums of CompuServe, you will likely find America Online a cakewalk, even in your early days.

If you venture into the special interest groups or online forums, take a while to look at how people interact with each other, then jump in. Also, let your fellow users know that you are new to the system or new to on-line forums. Generally speaking you will find helpful people who remember what it was like when they were new.

WHERE IS THIS CYBER-SHIP HEADING?

Overall, branching out to electronic online services is a rewarding experience. There are many information resources as well as friendships to be found. Electronic friends do not judge you by appearance, race, or gender. They judge you by what you say and how you say it. That makes for an interesting contrast to our day-to-day relationships.

Also, there is enormous opportunities to learn with electronic access. There is a wealth of information out there—practically every fact, every topic ever written—all you have to do is go find it.

For the next few years, you will probably need to become multi-service-lingual. Although, at first blush, it looks like all commercial services offer the same thing, look again—they do not.

As both the Internet and commercial online services evolve, I look for today's lines and categories to blur even more. Soon, you will be able to find almost anything and anyone online.

Happy hunting.

10

Desktop Video Conferencing: So You Want To Be In Movies?

Lights, camera, action! Most business people never dreamed that they would be sitting in front of a camera as a part of their day-to-day business life. Today's video-conferencing technology is changing all that. People find that the technology is convenient and cost-effective. In some cases, it is almost as easy as making a telephone call—except you can see the other person, share printed and annotated information, and more importantly, use technology to humanize communication. But, do not dismiss this technology as a picture phone; its uses go much further.

Video conferencing technology is destined to change a lot of careers. Why? Because it lets people change key components, namely who, where, and how work gets done.

For all its benefits, there are a few potentially negative issues wrought by this new technology. For example, many people suffer severe stage fright. As kids, they never liked having their pictures taken and the mere sight of a camera gets them fumbling. Further, the technology is still relatively new and many people do not know exactly when (or when not) to use video as a part of the work process.

This chapter is aimed at helping you learn more about the joys of video-conferencing technology, focusing on desktop video-conferencing systems and applications. It will also provide a few tips to help you avoid camera jitters.

I will start with a quick discussion about the basics of video conferencing and segment the different types and uses. If you have never considered using video conferencing, I will give you a few examples how others have harnessed the technology in innovative ways. Hopefully, the examples will serve as an idea generator for you.

Then, I will cover tips and techniques about how to behave, what to wear, and how to prepare. Even if you are an old hand at video conferences, this chapter should help you take the right steps to make you comfortable when cameras join the conference.

BUT FIRST: WHAT IS VIDEO CONFERENCING?

Video conferencing technology includes computer, television, and voice systems designed for general conference, classroom, or desktop use. If used constructively, video conferencing can eliminate (or at least significantly reduce) the need for business travel. And, it can change around certain jobs and staffing requirements.

Up until recently, the only options for video conferencing were costly and required months of planning to install. Companies in the 1980s spent upwards of $150,000 per room to properly equip it with cameras, speakers, special telephone lines, and even specially colored paint for the walls.

The technology for traditional boardroom-style video conferencing consisted of the following components:

- One or more speaker phones and television cameras aimed at speakers in conference rooms in several remote locations, say in different U.S. cities.
- Special (sometimes dedicated) voice and video communications circuits activated among the collaborating conferees at the participating conference room locations.
- A control system that lets you set up and control access to conference rooms or classrooms.
- An agenda and schedule for presentations and discussions by the video conferees. This may consist of slide presentations, conference notes, and other materials prepared and available to the conferees attending the teleconference. Some systems required a separate camera for presenting the visuals.

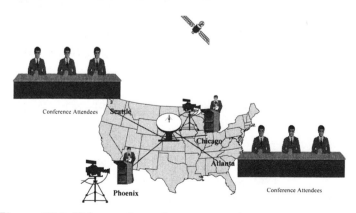

Figure 10.1. Video-conferencing components.

Types of Video Conferencing Systems

Today there are many more options for video conferencing. Low-cost desktop systems, some that run over normal telephone lines, have opened up the market for both new uses and users.

I divide the video conferencing technology into three basic categories: room, stage, and desktop.

- Room conferencing is the old-style formal conference room format. New technology, however, has brought down the stratospheric prices for this option to about $10,000–20,000 per location.
- My second category, stage conferencing, is the category for primarily one-way presentations. This involves setting up one location with a camera and formal presentation atmosphere and allowing remote locations to view the stage. If remote locations want to interact with the presenter, they would do it via telephone. As such, only the presenter's location needs to be fully decked out with camera gear.
- The third category is desktop video-conferencing systems. Depending on what you buy, you can have it up and running in about twenty minutes for less than $1,000 per location. Sure, you will make some quality compromises—the camera quality is not perfect and the video transmission is a little jerky, but it is nonetheless acceptable for a variety of business applications.

See Table 10.1 for the different types of video conferencing and what the configurations and uses are.

Category	Typical Configuration	Use
Room conferencing	For both recording and receiving: board room or a conference room specially set up with cameras, microphones	Long distance meetings with both or all sides participating interactively
Stage conferencing	Stage, class room, or a conference room specially set up with cameras, microphones for recording. Receiving can take place in a class room, auditorium, or specially equipped desktop.	Broadcast, long-distance learning, product presentations. Can be taped or live
Desktop video	For both recording and receiving: a specially equipped desktop PC	Interactive meetings and conferences. Usually small groups or one-to-one

Table 10.1. Different types of video conferencing available today.

Some systems offer fax and printer connection capabilities that allow conferees to exchange written documents during the conference. Newer systems allow for sharing a whiteboard or an application such as a word processor across a computer screen where people from each location can see the visuals. You can project images on slides for large audience viewing. Conferees can mark up draft copies of documents and save revisions.

EXAMPLES OF VIDEO INNOVATION

The versatility of video conferencing is its application to business, government, and education, with increasing amounts of productivity and cost savings. Businesses and government can save by rethinking who and where work must get done. Educators find a new way to spread knowledge.

Instant Credit

To give you an idea of how businesses can change around job functions, look to the innovative test created by electronics retailer Best Buy. To give customers instant credit cards, the chain is testing an interactive kiosk to replace in-store credit specialists. Instead of having a specialist on duty in each store, Best Buy and its partner Beneficial Finance created a video conference application with Intel's ProShare Developers Kit. The kiosk lets customers have a real time interactive conversation with a credit specialist, and if approved, prints a temporary picture-coded credit card for the customer to use on the spot.

If successful, retailers like Best Buy can choose to relocate some of the in-store work to a central location and free up the store staff to handle other customer service duties. This test could have a major impact on how all retailers give credit cards to new customers.

The One-Minute Mortgage (almost!)

It used to take months for people to apply and be approved for a home loan. Desktop video conferencing is changing all that. Consider the test started by Countrywide Credit Industries in mid-1995. Using Intel's low cost ProShare desktop video conferencing system, home buyers and lenders can get together electronically. The mortgage origination system starts at Virtual Realty Network, Inc., which routes the video call from brokers' offices to Countrywide or one of eleven other lenders involved in the test. The borrower can negotiate with the loan officer, close the deal, and submit the loan application, all via video conference. The mortgage loan is not approved on the spot, but having all the information put together in the format the lender needs will undoubtedly compress the approval time.

On the work side, this development could rewrite the rules for the real estate and mortgage loan business. If the mortgage officer is only a video-call away, it does not matter if he or she resides in the same city, state, or time zone. This could open up a new level of competition for the industry. It could also rearrange the jobs of loan officials. Since it does not matter where the loan officer physically resides, a large lender, like Countrywide, could choose to centralize all loan application people to one office, or disperse them to home offices.

Government Video Conferencing

Government agencies, such as NASA, have been using video conferencing for nearly a decade. At NASA headquarters, and as many as fifteen centers around the United States, video conferencing is used to exchange audio, video, computer data, and computer graphics information. The video system is linked via satellite and telephone land lines. This NASA-wide Video Teleconferencing System (ViTS) is a Compression Labs Inc. (CLI) system that uses analog to video conversion technology. At the Johnson Space Center many times a day, NASA employees use six ViTS conference rooms that can employ two simultaneous video systems. Top NASA executives' conference rooms can also be switched on to use ViTS or Voice Teleconferencing System (VoTS), a voice-only system. NASA estimates 40 to 50 percent of the participants in this program save tax payers' thousands of dollars in travel costs each year with just 75-percent utilization of the ViTS facilities.

Impact on Education

Full-motion, two-way video conferencing technology can have a dramatic impact on distance learning. It can bring the teacher to remote locations. For example, North Slope Borough needed to deliver high school mathematics and art courses to students in outlying villages spread across 88,000 square miles in Alaska. They use teleconferencing systems with cameras and monitors that are fully interactive so students and teachers in distant locations can see each other and talk to each other as if in the same room.

Several years ago, Texas A&M University at College Station, Texas, started using video conferencing among twenty-three locations with image capture and annotation using VideoTelecom's MediaConferencing and Pen Pal Graphics systems. The cost savings are in reduced travel time for college administrators and faculty, enhanced communications between members of the Texas A&M University System (TAMUS) around the state, and the ability to teach courses simultaneously at several TAMUS campuses.

As video conferencing becomes affordable to schools it could be used to connect kids learning Spanish in a Texas school with those learning English in Mexico to let them hear each other talk in their native language and learned languages. This direct contact can help the children learn more than just the language, it gives them a chance to understand the culture of their foreign neighbors and develop a good sense of other parts of the world.

Where Is it Going?

So, if you find yourself asking "Where is it going?" you are not alone. Analysts can only speculate how fast and how far video conferencing will spread through many work environments. It could have enormous impact on selection of work teams, telecommuting, and all kinds of other issues. I think it will also turn into technology used as a competitive weapon. Imagine how it could leverage human assets in an organization. This technology is going to benefit a lot of people. Stay tuned.

TIPS FOR HOW TO DRESS AND BEHAVE ON CAMERA

So, with all the world looking at innovative uses of video conferencing systems, it might just be a matter of time before you get your chance in front of a camera. What do you do? How do you prepare?

Just like a live presentation, you want to look your best. You want to project a confident, competent image. Consider the following tips for both desktop and presentation-style video conferences:

- **Wear pastel colors.** It is better to wear a pastel blouse/shirt and suit rather than a dark suit and white blouse/shirt. The great contrast between the dark and light clothing fights with the camera, especially low-cost desktop video cameras that tend to be lower quality than professional gear. Lighter pastel colors near your skin will make it easier for the camera to focus. They are much better for video conferencing.
- **Wear appropriate clothing.** If you are conducting your video conference from a casual location, make sure you can get to a quick wardrobe change. For example, a friend of mine who uses video conferencing from his home office, always keeps a clip-on tie and sports jacket nearby. If he is called into a video

meeting with clients or company managers, he opens his desk drawer, puts on his tie, and turns on the camera.

- **Buy a goose neck lamp.** Your office may not have optimum lighting for desktop video cameras, but lighting problems are easy to correct if you have a low-cost, small goose neck lamp. Use the type with a small halogen bulb for best results. The light is intense, but cool. You will not feel like you are on stage with bright lights blaring in front of your eyes.
- **Look at the camera.** If you have a point to make, find the camera, and look directly into the lens.

Figure 10.2. Look directly at the camera for best eye contact.

- **Watch your signals; body language counts.** Lean forward in your chair during the conference, this will make you appear interested and alert.
- **Don't fiddle.** Follow your mother's manners for the dinner table: no elbows on the table, and if you have a tendency to play with objects be sure all are out of your reach.

- **Arrange your screen.** Most desktop video conferencing software let you place or move pictures and objects anywhere on the screen. Try putting the picture of the other party near the camera. For example, if the camera is located on top of the monitor on

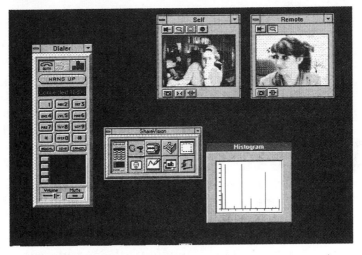

Figure 10.3. If you move the picture of the remote person (as well as your own) just underneath your camera, it will help you talk to the camera and give you a more natural look.

the right side, then place the picture of the remote party in the upper right side of the screen and place your picture next to the remote party. This way your eyes will stay focused at the other person and you'll look more natural.

- **Practice, practice, practice!** If you are going to do a standup presentation, then you need to practice it just like you would for a public seminar. If you are participating as part of a panel, make sure you prepare yourself to discuss the assigned topic. Even if it is just a desktop video conference, check your camera to make sure the lighting and color look good.
- **Speak slowly and clearly.** And, while you are practicing, use your best speaking voice and practice in front of the camera when no one else is present.

Usually you can arrange with the person who runs the video conferencing control room to let you record a talk and view it afterwards, or bring your own camera or tape recorder. You will notice that your voice will change a little from normal tones. It usually gets lower and louder.

- **Use cues.** If you are making a video presentation, very little is hidden. If you need cue cards or a list to prompt you, record your practice session and move your eyes so it does not appear that you are reading. For presentations or large conferences, more than one camera may be used; so make sure the conference controller does not switch on a camera that shows the cue cards.

- **Set up carefully.** Ask the participants to sit within camera range so they can be seen at the other locations. Some systems use audio switching, which means that the camera will switch to the site where someone is speaking. This means loud extraneous conversation among participants might cause the camera to switch to another site.

- **Practice more.** Practice using the graphics camera to show information before your class or meeting begins.

- **Arrive early.** If you are the chairperson or instructor, you should arrive early to make sure everything is set up correctly. Even for informal desktop video conferences, turn on your camera and check lighting and angle adjustments so you feel comfortable and do not fiddle once the conference starts.

BUYING A VIDEO CONFERENCING SYSTEM?

If you were standing in the wrong place and were selected to help buy your company's video conferencing system, let me offer you condolences. This is no easy task. Now, let me give you a few words of advice.

First, make no assumptions. Video conferencing systems do not inter-operate like telephones. If your friends use an Intel ProShare system, and you own a Creative Labs ShareVision, chances are that you will not be able to conference (yet). While standards are being developed, many existing systems have had to develop products before the standards were set.

Moreover, the technology, especially for desktop systems, changes daily so you will have to make sure you read up on the latest technology advancements in magazines or other periodicals. Do not just take the advice of the first salesperson that you meet who can correctly spell video.

We are approaching a day and time where your business card will carry just one more line of data: your video conferencing number. So, get ready to print cards with your phone, fax, pager, cellular phone, e-mail address, and desktop video conferencing number! (Let's hope the technology develops that allows people to use one number for everything.)

Tips for Buying Desktop Video Conferencing

Desktop video systems have a few peculiar requirements, so be sure to check the specifics of the units you consider. The primary requirements to look for are: what type of communications standards do they follow, do they support multi-point conferences, and what upgrades are planned.

- **Check communications requirements.** Many desktop systems require you to install special high-speed communications lines called Integrated Services Digital Network SDN). These lines are now available in major metropolitan areas, but double-check before you assume you can put them at every location. Also, check for installation rates and monthly charges, which vary widely by region. For example, on the West Coast people can readily get

ISDN lines for little (if any) installation costs and less than $30 per month. By contrast, people in the Southwest must pay a $578 per line installation fee and $58 per month (as of this writing).

- **Use a meter with local conferences.** Some desktop systems let you video conference across your existing office local area network. This is a boon to would-be users, but often a fear for network administrators. Since video conferencing can gobble up lots of the communication lines, special monitoring software should be used to make sure you do not overdo the communications.

- **Buy systems with smarts.** Look for a desktop video conferencing system that uses intelligence. For example, Creative's ShareVision uses extreme compression that takes a user's voice, video image, and computer data (like shared white board or application screens) and crunches it with a compression ratio of 350:1. Also, intelligent systems figure out a priority of what to transmit across the lines. Some systems will give the first priority to voice (so users do not have to stop talking), then to data, and finally to video.

- **Watch out for standards.** The International Telecommunications Union (ITU), the same United Nations organization who developed standards for fax machines and modems, is developing a standard for video communications. The standard for video conferencing over ISDN lines is H.320 and the new standard for plain old telephone systems (POTS) is H.324. A forthcoming standard, T.120, will allow information sharing that will govern a shared work area so that several people can work on something at the same time.

Tips for Buying Large Video Conferencing Systems

Large video conferencing systems have their own unique requirements. Here is a list of important questions to ask when selecting a room-sized video conferencing system:

- Do you need technicians at each site during a video conference? If the system requires an on-site technician, the costs go up. Moreover, you have to consider training for these technicians and backup people in case of illness.
- How many monitors will you need at each location and how many viewers will they accommodate?
- What will the layout of the conference rooms or classrooms be like? Sometimes the rooms cannot accommodate the equipment needs such as the camera's horizontal field of view.
- Where will the audio come from—monitor speakers in the front, overhead speakers, or monitors in the back?
- What size groups are going to use the video conferencing system and can the cameras, monitors, microphones, and image sizes accommodate them?
- How much can users tinker with the equipment?
- Can user initiated adjustments be limited so they do not cause serious interference with operations?
- What kind of on-site diagnostics will be available and how easy are they to access and read?

Lights, Camera, Action!

Setting up for a successful video conference takes planning and forethought. It is a little more work than just walking into a conference room, slapping down a notepad, and starting a meeting. But, video conferencing is an effective way of getting geographically disbursed people together to share their thoughts and ideas. With a little work, the experience can be almost like being there.

ARE YOU READY FOR THE ELECTRONIC ERA?

With this chapter, I am going to end my series of tips and tricks about specific technologies. The rest of the book is devoted to helping you figure out where you need to go from here. Take the office technology literacy quizzes in the next section. They are bound to tell you a little more about what you do and do not know. They should help point you in the right direction.

I also suggest that you glance through the glossary. Do you know all the terms? I gave you a short list intentionally so the glossary would not look so imposing. It is a good idea to master these terms because they will help as you do your own technology shopping in the future.

Next, let me suggest that you do not stop your study and reading with the this book. Let your interests take you to others. Also, take a look at the computer trade magazines for current up-to-the-minute views of what is going on. You should pursue the advertisements as well. That way you can keep a keen eye out for the latest information.

Last, let me give you one piece of advice. Technology can be both fun and frustrating—often at the same time. Sometimes it works, sometimes it does not. When you find technology that does not quite suit your needs, do not give up. Just regroup and look again. The industry is full of bright people trying to bring innovative products to your door. Let them in.

11

Literacy Quiz Level I: Computer Literacy

In Chapter 1, and elsewhere, I have made a big deal out of being computer literate. Actually, computer literacy is only part of the challenge. People need to be electronically literate, knowing the basics of fax, voice mail, and other gizmos. But, computer literacy is often the most elusive, so let's start here.

For computer literacy, this chapter presents a few basic questions and possible answers. Assume you work on a network connected PC running standard applications. This also includes a section for those who have begun to use Microsoft Windows as well as Windows 95.

To make things easier, the quiz is multiple choice. But, beware, there are a few trick questions, so read carefully. Choose the letter to the left of the answer that seems correct to you, then, when you are done, check out your answers at the end of this section. Since you don't have to turn your results into your teacher (or your boss) you should be encouraged to answer without peeking into the back of the section. Good luck.

1. How many characters (or letters) can you use to make up a file name?

    A. 8
    B. 11
    C. 14
    D. None of the above

2. The following file name would cause an error: CCC*01.DOC

    A. True
    B. False

3. Some application programs pre-assign file name extensions.

    A. True
    B. False

4. Diskettes come in two popular sizes: 3-1/2 inch and 5-1/4 inch. For each size, there are two types. What are they and do they require different disk drives?

    A. High-density and low-density. Each can be used in any disk drive as long as the drive supports the diskette size.
    B. High-density and low-density. High-density diskettes can only be read by high-density drives. Low-density diskettes can usually be read by either high- or low-density drives.
    C. High-density and low capacity. Both can be read by any type of drive that supports the diskette size.
    D. None of the above.

5. How can you tell if a 3-1/2 inch diskette is high-density?

    A. There is no visible sign.
    B. It is a different color.

C. There is generally a mark that says HD on the upper right side of the diskette.
D. None of the above.

6. What could potentially destroy all the data saved on a diskette?

   A. Exposing the diskette to a very warm climate.
   B. Carrying the diskette in an unprotected briefcase.
   C. Exposing the diskette to a magnet.
   D. All of the above.

7. How must a diskette be prepared before it is used?

   A. It must be labeled.
   B. It must be formatted.
   C. It must be labeled and formatted.
   D. None of the above

8. All PC-type computers start up on Drive C:

   A. True
   B. False

9. When a computer starts up, the first file it reads is called AUTOEXEC.BAT.

   A. True
   B. False

10. With either DOS or Windows commands, you can select the files in a subdirectory without knowing the name of its parent directory.

    A. True
    B. False

11. You can edit DOS or Windows command files with a generic word processing program.(Examples: AUTOEXEC.BAT, CONFIG.SYS, WIN.INI).

    A. Yes, however, you must save the file in a plain text (ASCII) format.
    B. Yes, there is no problem using any popular word processing program.
    C. No.

12. Printers can only be attached to a PC's parallel port.

A. True
B. False

13. The types of printers capable of printing full pictures and graphics include: laser printers, dot matrix printers, and impact (wheel or thimble) printers.

A. True
B. False

14. A modem is:

A. A device used to modulate RF signals from a computer.
B. A connector that fits on the back of a PC.
C. A device that lets your PC communicate over telephone wires.
D. None of the above.

15. BAUD (or BPS) refers to:

A. The speed of a modem.
B. The binary attributes of a file.
C. Cables.
D. None of the above.

16. Which is the largest file?

A. 7 GB
B. 14 MB
C. 2 KB
D. 16,000 bytes

17. If your computer has 4 MB of RAM, then you should be able to store at least 100 pages of text on its disk.

A. True
B. False
C. Answer unknown from facts supplied.

18. Most PCs today come with network attachments built-in.

A. False
B. True

19. Networks let people share files, printers, and other people's hard disks.

A. True
B. False

20. A spreadsheet file created with Lotus 1-2-3 cannot be used by another spreadsheet program, such as Excel or Quattro Pro.

A. True
B. False

21. A spreadsheet file saved on a network cannot be copied to a diskette.

A. True
B. False

22. Your computer can become infected with a computer virus if you log into a computer bulletin board system (BBS) and read messages.

A. True
B. False

23. Network drives, directories, and subdirectories can be set up as drive letters. As such, you might be able to refer to them as Drive G: or Drive Z:

A. True
B. False

24. The function keys on the keyboard always (or usually) refer to the same function in software packages.

A. True
B. False

25. PC software is licensed to the PC itself. If you have purchased a copy for your desktop PC at the office, you must also purchase a copy for your notebook PC, and another copy for your PC at home.

A. True
B. False

ANSWERS:

1. **B. is the correct answer for DOS and Windows 3.1 / D is the correct answer for Windows 95.** A DOS or Windows 3.1 file name can have a total of 11 characters, with eight in the beginning, then a period, and followed by a three-character extension. By contrast, if you use Windows 95, you can create file names with up to 255 characters and include spaces and just about any character.

2. **A. True.** For DOS, Windows 3.1, and Windows 95, you can use numbers and some special characters to make up a file name, you cannot use the asterisk (*) as one of them. Your file name can consist of the letters A–Z (if you use lowercase, they will be converted to upper-case); the digits 0–9; or the special characters _, ^, $, ~, !, #, %, &, -, {, }, (,), @, ~, `, '. File names cannot include periods (except to denote the extension), and cannot use commas. For Windows 95, you are free to use any goofy character you choose except \, /, *, ?, <, >, |.

3. **A. True.** A number of applications pre-assign a three-character extension to the file name so it will be easier to identify the file. For example, Microsoft's Excel will append a .XLS to whatever file name you give it. You can, however, change the extension, but I do not recommend it. Many utility software packages, such as the Windows File Manager or Windows 95 Explorer, use the extension as a way of knowing what application to launch and use with certain files.

4. **B.** There are high-density and low-density diskettes and drives. A low-density drive cannot read a diskette formatted as a high-density. While most new computers today use only high-density drives, you may have others around the office or in early model laptop computers. Be careful when using the older drives; they

cannot reliably read or write to a high-density diskette. If you try to force it you can scramble your data.

5. **C.** Diskette manufacturers have been very consistent
about telling users what they are using. There is a
mark HD on the upper right side of high-density 3-1/2
inch diskettes.

6. **C.** A magnet will potentially scramble all the data on
your diskette. Be careful! Keep your diskettes away
from any magnetic field; that includes magnetic paper
clip holders; telephone receivers; and little kitchen re-
frigerator paper holders. They can be lethal to your
data.

7. **B.** Diskettes must be formatted but labeling them is
optional. Some diskettes can be purchased as pre-
formatted. Otherwise, you must use the FORMAT
command from DOS (or choose Format Disk... from
the Disk menu in the Windows File Manager or Windows 95 Explorer).

8. **B. False.** If your computer has a diskette drive
(designated as Drive A:) your computer will look there
first and try to load any operating system it finds. If
there is no diskette in Drive A: (or the diskette drive
door is open) and you have a fixed disk set up as Drive
C: it will try to load the operating system from there.

9. **B. False.** The computer will first read the file called
CONFIG.SYS and load any device drivers, make any
drive assignments, or perform other instructions in
that file. After it completes loading the instructions of
CONFIG.SYS, it then begins to execute the instructions from AUTOEXEC.BAT.

10. **B. False.** You must either select (or at least, know
the name) of the directory before you can get to files in
a subdirectory. For that reason, it is important to
know where you are saving your files. You might not
find it too easy to locate the file that is buried down
several subdirectories deep. (There are, however,
commercial and third-party utilities that will find a
file anywhere on the fixed disk.)

11. **A.** You can use any word-processing program or text editor that is capable of saving a file in straight ASCII text. If you don't specify this format, your word processor may add special characters or formatting codes that could cause problems. Be careful about editing any file that your computer uses for hardware or software configuration. One wrong character in the wrong place and you could be out of luck.

12. **B. False.** Most printers are attached to a parallel port but in some cases they can be attached to a computer's serial port, or a network fileserver, or a print server, or directly to a network wire.

13. **B. False.** Printers with wheels or thimbles cannot produce pictures or graphics. (There are not many of these around anymore.) Printers that use ink jet, dot matrix, laser, or thermal transfer can all print graphics just fine.

14. **C.** A modem is a device that lets your computer communicate over telephone wires. Depending on the type, it can be externally attached to one of the computer's serial ports, placed in one of the expansion slots inside the PC, or slipped into the PCMCIA (or PC Card) slot of a portable computer.

15. **A.** Baud or (BPS) refers to the speed of a modem or telephone transmission of data. Popular baud rates for modems today are 2,400, 9,600, 14.4K, and 28.8K bits per second (BPS). Baud is an older term and refers to a speed that is almost one bit per second.

16. **A.** 7 GB (gigabytes) is larger than any of the other file sizes. The smallest unit is a byte, which is approximately one character. A KB (kilobyte) is 1024 characters. A MB (megabyte) is approximately 1,000 KB. A GB (gigabyte) is approximately 1,000 MB.

17. **C.** The answer is unknown from the facts supplied. RAM (random access memory) refers to the amount of volatile memory a computer has for processing applications and data and has nothing to do with disk space.

cations and data and has nothing to do with disk space.

18. **A. False.** Although most business PCs end up on networks, a network interface card (NIC) usually has to be added. The NIC fits into one of the expansion slots inside a standard desktop. Some desktop PCs, such as the Compaq DeskPro, build in the network adapter and no additional add-on card is required. Alternatively, there are network devices, such as the Xircom, which attach to the parallel port of a PC or notebook computer. These devices come in handy for portable computers that may not be on the network at all times.

19. **B. False.** While networks are popular configurations for people to share files and printers, they do not necessarily allow sharing of other people's hard disks. Many network configurations use file servers and let people share disk space on the server, but not each other's personal hard disks.

20. **B. False.** Most spreadsheet programs can easily read, manipulate, or update a file created by Lotus 1-2-3. There may be a few formatting characters which will not be accessible by other software programs, but the data will be accessible.

21. **B. False.** Files can be easily copied from network drives to local hard disks or diskettes. Unless someone has put on sophisticated software to block copying, there is no problem.

22. **B. False.** Simply reading messages on a computer bulletin board will not expose you to a virus. You would need to fully execute a program to be exposed. Albeit, it is a good idea to run a virus checker on a regular basis if you are a frequent modem user.

23. **A. True.** Network drives, under most operating systems, will let you configure both directories and subdirectories as a drive letter. In the Novell NetWare environment, a network drive by the name of SERVER1/SYS:DATA/SALES/REPORTS can be given

the name of G:, for example. That way, anytime you needed to get to the subdirectory, you could avoid having to type in the long subdirectory description.

24. **B. False.** Although software publishers are trying to show consistency in mapping functions to function keys, there are no real standards.

25. **B. False.** All PC software licenses are not created equal. Depending on the software publisher, the type of software package, and seemingly, the day of the week, you may or may not be able to make legal copies of the software for multiple computers. Check each software package (and each version) to be sure. Software licensing has become a complicated area to track and vendors frequently change their policies from release to release. Read the fine print carefully.

SCORING:

For each correct answer, give yourself four points. Add up your score and then compare it with the following table:

0–32   **Pathetic.** You better find adult supervision whenever you turn on your PC. Find a remedial PC class pronto. Read books geared for "dummies," buy elementary videos, and chase down a computer coach. You could be dangerous driving a PC all by yourself.

33–64   **Better, but not great.** You should consider taking some courses or reading a few books or viewing videos. You are off to a start, but need to further your knowledge.

65–84   **Average and on the way.** You have got the basic concepts down but probably have Swiss cheese knowledge—solid in some places but plenty of holes. Look at the questions that you missed and target your studies on those areas. Keep learning.

85–100   **Great.** You can keep the keys to your PC.

12

Literacy Quiz Level II: Fax & Voice Mail

Chapters 4 and 5 deal with fax machines and voice mail, and the impact that they are having on the business world and society. As these technologies continue to grow, it is important to understand where these technologies came from, how they work, and where they are going.

To test your knowledge of voice mail and fax technologies, take the following quiz. You will be tested on hardware, software, and current philosophies of how they are best used. Good luck.

1. Plain paper fax machines are the cheapest available fax option.

   A. True
   B. False

2. The biggest problem with a fax is:

   A. Finding the time to send a fax.
   B. With no fax communication standard, fax hardware varies greatly and is not compatible.
   C. Faxing only contributes to the amount of paper in the office.
   D. Faxing costs more to send than it does to mail a letter.

3. Which is the most common type of fax setup in use today?

   A. The PC fax.
   B. The stand-alone fax.
   C. The printer fax option card.

4. The PC Fax machine views the incoming fax as:

   A. An ASCII text file to be saved to the hard disk.
   B. An ASCII text file to be sent to the printer.
   C. A graphic image, usually with a PCX or TIF format.
   D. A file, each with a unique code for identification purposes.

5. In order to combat the limitations of graphics file conversion, many vendors are:

   A. Using faster, more expensive chips to speed the conversion process.
   B. Developing hardware that will break up faxes into "blocks" for faster processing.
   C. Limiting the amount of graphics allowed in each transmission.

D. Using OCR technology to convert the incoming fax into a text file.

6. Sending or receiving a PC Fax cannot be done in the background. Users must wait until the fax takes over all system resources.

   A. True
   B. False

7. For a business producing mostly computer-generated output, the best fax option choice would be:

   A. Use of a printer fax option card.
   B. A stand-alone fax machine.
   C. A networked PC fax that handles the routing of incoming and outgoing faxes.

8. The fastest growing segment of the fax market is the:

   A. PC fax machine.
   B. The stand-alone fax machine.
   C. The printer option card fax machine.

9. Which of the following is not a "school of thought" as to where faxes are headed in the future?

   A. Faxes will become obsolete and no one will use them.
   B. Faxes will evolve into an e-mail-only format.
   C. Faxes will continue, unabated, well into the next century.
   D. Faxes will replace the U.S. Postal Service.

10. A fax cover sheet:

    A. Is essential with an informal fax.
    B. Does nothing but cause increased telephone charges.

C. Is the best way to make sure the fax was delivered properly.

11. Which of the following is not a benefit of voice mail?

   A. Cuts down on long-distance telephone charges.
   B. Eliminates the missed call; all messages reach their destination, not a secretary.
   C. Conveys emotion not capable in a letter or fax.
   D. Long reports can be dictated for a permanent record.

12. Voice mail is a cheaper alternative to the fax.

   A. True
   B. False

13. When leaving a voice mail greeting, convey as much information to the caller as possible.

   A. True
   B. False

14. Some voice mail systems allow the caller to request notifications be sent to a remote pager.

   A. True
   B. False

15. Call accounting systems offered by some voice mail systems:

   A. Can help establish controls for measurement of incoming and outgoing calls.
   B. Automate the payment process with the accounting department.
   C. Can record employee's long-distance telephone conversations.

16. Which of the following is not a disadvantage of voice mail systems?

A. Proliferation of voice messages quickly eats up disk space.

B. Voice messages cannot be skimmed to see which are important, which are not.

C. Long, detailed messages make getting the point across difficult.

D. Correspondence takes place at different times.

17. Which of the following is not a problem with forwarding voice messages to others?

    A. Proliferation of disk space.

    B. Possible security violations.

    C. All messages are not crucial to all people, wasting time is wasting money.

    D. Everyone stays informed, quickly and efficiently.

18. The future of voice mail lies with merging voice, text, video, and sound into a very effective multimedia tool.

    A. True
    B. False

19. Fax technology has been around for more than sixty years.

    A. True
    B. False

20. If your fax card sends a fax at 14,400 bps, and the receiving fax can only receive at 9,600 bps, the fax is sent at 9,600 bps.

    A. True
    B. False

ANSWERS:

1. **B. False.** Plain paper fax machines are not the cheapest available fax option. The machines themselves cost more than fax machines using conventional fax paper. Although the cost of the plain paper machine is greater when compared to the conventional machine, paper costs are lower in the long run with a plain paper fax.

2. **C.** The biggest single problem with faxes today is the proliferation of paper. Receiving a fax on thermal fax paper requires the receiver to copy the fax onto plain paper to file away in a file folder. Because faxes fade with time, copying is essential. Further, some people misuse fax when they should send documents in e-mail. Too often people end up rekeying information that came from a computer through fax right back into another computer on the other end.

3. **B.** The most common type of fax setup today by far and away is the stand-alone fax machine. Although other fax setups account for great growth, the old stand-alone is still the most common. (That needs to change. Old-style fax machines do not offer the same productivity benefits as newer PC fax options.)

4. **C.** The PC Fax machine views incoming faxes as graphics files (*.pcx or *.tif). A fax machine "scans" the paper and converts the text and/or pictures into a graphics file to be transmitted across the phone line. The receiving fax machine then simply converts the graphics file and prints the fax.

5. **D.** Because the conversion process of the fax process is so slow, software vendors have developed Optical Character Recognition (OCR) technology that converts the incoming graphics file into either a standard text file or a word processing file. The text file or specific word-processing file can then be viewed and printed quickly. The OCR software also greatly reduces the size of the converted file, thus saving precious disk space.

6. **B. False.** Most fax software performs transparently in the "background." That is, users are not aware that the fax board is making system resource requests. The fax is sent or received, with no apparent interruption to the user.

7. **C.** For a business producing mostly computer-generated output, the networked PC Fax is the most sensible choice. Instead of printing the document and walking over to the fax machine, users can send the document over the networked PC Fax without ever leaving their chair, or printing a piece of paper. Not only is paper saved, but transmission times are generally faster because the document is already an electronic image.

8. **A.** The fastest growing segment of the fax market is that of the PC Fax. With most of the world's faxes coming from the computer world, companies are finding that it makes sense to send them via the computer. In addition, mass faxes (similar to mass mailings) do not require a human supervisor. The PC Fax will take care of all of the details without wasting anyone's time.

9. **D.** The U.S. Postal Service is in no fear of being replaced by the fax. Although the movement is

toward electronic mail, some people do not have fax or computer hardware. The Post Office will continue to deliver. Some people believe that faxes will become nonexistent as the masses move to a cheaper electronic mail. Most believe the fax machine will remain, although a greater emphasis will be placed on e-mail.

10. **C.** The fax cover sheet is essential, especially in the business world. To ensure proper delivery, and make sure the entire fax was transmitted, a cover sheet is a must.

11. **D.** Long reports with a lot of details are often lost in the shuffle of voice mail. Voice mail was intended to facilitate the message-taking function, not the report function. Long reports are best delivered in hard copy form.

12. **B. False.** Voice mail is a more expensive alternative than the fax in the short run. Initial set-up costs in hardware and initial training tend to be greater than purchasing and training employees for a fax machine. In the long run, with paper and labor costs associated with permanent forms of correspondence, voice mail is actually cheaper.

13. **B. False.** Voice mail greetings should be concise and to the point. Long greetings turn off the listener, and make him/her reluctant to leave a message. Greetings should be limited to name and extension with a possible reason as to absence. The last and most important aspect of the greeting is a sincere plea to leave a detailed message.

14. **A. True.** Being constantly informed can be the difference between success and failure. Some voice systems enable users to leave a message and then request the receiver of the call be paged, so the business person is never out of touch.

15. **A.** Call accounting systems can help establish controls about the volume of calls being processed, who is getting the most calls, and who is making the most calls. After all, if the calls cannot be measured, they cannot be managed.

16. **D.** The whole purpose of a voice mail system is so that communication can take place at different times. Voice mail eliminates "phone tag." Callers know their message will be heard. Receivers of messages know they have been contacted. With international offices, voice mail can be a convenient way to communicate across time zones.

17. **D.** The main benefit of forwarding messages is so that everyone stays informed of changing situations quickly. Separate memos do not have to be typed. Correspondence is automatic.

18. **A. True.** Multimedia is the future of all communications, not just voice mail. The trend is to merge voice, data, text, and sound into a powerful tool. As hardware performance increases and prices come down, more and more people will make the move to multimedia.

19. **A. True.** Fax technology has been around for more than sixty years. However, until the 1980s it was treated like nothing more than advanced Morse code. Its main benefit, instant access to

information, was not utilized. Faxes often sat in mail rooms for days waiting to be delivered. The advantages of fax technology were not realized until fax prices came into reach for everyone.

20. A. True. Faxes can only be sent at the rate the receiving machine can handle. If the sending machine is capable of 14.4k bps, and the receiving machine can handle only 9,600 bps, transmission occurs at the slower of the two rates.

SCORING:

For each correct answer, give yourself 5 points. Add up your score and then compare it with the following table:

0–2   **Pathetic.** Do not touch anything! Your lack of knowledge probably cannot hurt anything, but ask for help before you act. Read beginner's books and spend some time watching and learning from others in the office. If not, hit the books. You could be dangerous even trying to fax a document.

33–64   **Better, but no prize.** You know enough to be dangerous, but not enough to get yourself out of any trouble you get into. Read more books and be careful. You are off to a start, but you need to further your knowledge.

65–84   **Average and on the way.** You have got the basic concepts down but probably have Swiss cheese knowledge—solid in some places but plenty of holes. Look at the questions that you missed and target your studies on those areas. Keep listening and learning!

85–100   **Great!** You can keep the keys to the office.

APPENDIX

A

Product Reference Guide

Action Technologies
1301 Marina Village Pkwy #100
Alameda, CA 94501
510/521-6190
WorkFlow

AT&T Paradyne
8545 126th Avenue North
Largo, FL 34649-2826
800/482-3333
EasyLink

America Online
America Online, Inc.
8619 Westwood Center Dr.
Vienna, VA 22182
800/227-6364 Fax: 703/883-1509
Online service for Macintosh and Apple II Users

AMIX
American Information Exchange
2345 Yale St.
Palo Alto, CA 94306
415/856-1234 Fax: 415/856-4123
Electronic marketplace for buying and selling information
and consulting services

Bix
BYTE Magazine, McGraw-Hill
One Phoenix Mill Lane
Peterborough, NH 03458
603/924-9281 Fax: 603/924-2530
News, vendor support, special interest groups of PC users

BRS After Dark
BRS Information Technologies
800 Westpark Dr.
McLean, VA 22102
800/289-4277 Fax: 703/893-4632
Most popular databases from BRS Search Services at
reduced evening rates.

BRS Search Service
BRS Information Technologies
800 Westpark Dr.
McLean, VA 22102
800/289-4277 Fax: 703/893-4632

CallWare Technologies
2323 Foothill Drive
Salt Lake City, UT 84109
800/888-4226

Canon
Home Office Products Division
Lake Success, NY 11042
516/328-4757 Fax: 516/328-4769

Citrix Systems, Inc.
210 University Drive, Suite 700
Coral Springs, FL 33071
305/755-0559 Fax: 305/341-6880
WinFrame™ for Networks

Compaq Computer Corporation
20555 State Highway 249
Houston, TX 77070-2698
713/370-0670
Computer manufacturer

Comp-U-Store
CUC Int'l. Inc.
7070 Summer St.
Stanford, CT 06901
800/843-7777
Online shopping from 250,000 brand names

Compression Labs Inc.
2860 Junction Avenue
San Jose, CA 95134-1900
408/435-3000
Video communications products

CompuServe Information Services
CompuServe, Inc.
P.O. Box 20212
Columbus, OH 43220
800/848-8199 Fax: 614/457-0348
E-mail, news, forums, home shopping, games financial
and reference data, CompuServe Viewer™

CompuServe Mail
CompuServe, Inc.
P.O. Box 20212
Columbus, OH 43220
800/848-8199 Fax: 614/457-0348
E-mail to CompuServe subscribers and large
corporations; interconnections to other e-mail services

Connect Information Service
Connect, Inc.
10161 Bubb Rd.
Cupertino, CA 95014
408/973-0110 Fax: 408/973-0497
E-mail for Macintosh and MS-DOS computers

Coris
Thompson Financial Network
11 Farnsworth St.
Boston, MA 02210
617/345-2000
Business information and news

Creative Labs, Inc.
1901 McCarthy Blvd.
Milpitas, CA 95035
408/428-6600
Desktop video conferencing and CD-ROM drives
Phone Blaster/Sound Blaster

Data Communications
Syscom Inc.
2362-D Qume Dr.
San Jose, CA 95131
408/432-8153
E-mail, computer-to-fax and computer-to-telex services

Data Resources
Data Resources Inc.
24 Hartwell Ave
Lexington, MA 02173
617/863-5100
Financial, economic, and industrial information

Data-Star
D-S Marketing Inc.
485 Devon Park Dr., Ste. 110
Wayne, PA 19087
215/ 687-6777 Fax: 215/ 687-0984
International online information: business, medicine,
engineering, pharmaceutical and environmental

DataTimes
14000 Quail Springs Pkwy., Ste. 450
Oklahoma City, OK 73134
405/751-6400 Fax: 405/755-8028
Text of regional and national newspapers, two wire
services, and Dow Jones News/Retrieval

Delphi
General Videotex Corp.
1030 Massachusetts Ave., 4th Fl.
Cambridge, MA 02138-5302
617/491-3393 Fax: 617/491-6642
Business and financial services, news travel services,
online shopping, conferencing, member forums,
and downloadable software

Delrina Corporation
895 Don Mills
500-2 Park Centre
Toronto, Ontario, M3C 1W3, Canada
416/441-3676
FormFlow

DIALOG
DIALOG Information Services, Inc.
3460 Hillview Ave.
Palo Alto, CA 94304
415/858-3785 Fax: 415/858-7069
Many services such as DIALOG Business and Corporate
Connection, DIALMIAL E-mail, DIALOGLINK PC soft-
ware, and KNOWLEDGE INDEX

Direct Shop
Wescom Corp.
333 Jericho Turnpike
Jericho, NY 11753
516/433-3770
Online shopping from over 500,000 products and services

Dow Jones News/Retrieval
Dow Jones & Company, Inc.
P.O. Box 300
Princeton, NJ 08543-0300
609/520-8349 Fax: 609/520-4660
Up-to-the-minute business/financial news and information about companies, markets, and industries

EAASY SABRE
American Airlines Inc.
P.O. Box 619616, MD 1254
DFW Airport, TX 75261
800/433-7556
Reservations at over 600 airlines, 20,000 hotels, and 50 car rental agencies

Electronic Mail
CompuServe, Inc.
P.O. Box 20212
Columbus, OH 43220
800/848-8199
Online shopping from a variety of merchants

Epic Service
Online Computer Library Center (OCLC)
6565 Frantz Rd.
Dublin, OH 43017-0702
614/764-6000
Bibliographic, indexing, and abstracting information

Ericsson GE Mobile Communications, Inc.
45C Commerce Way
Totowa, NJ 07512-1154
201/890-3600
Communications products

General Magic
2465 Latham Street #100
Mountain View, CA 94040
415/965-0400
Personal communications, Magic Cap

GEnie
General Electric Information Services, Inc.
401 N. Washington St.
Rockville, MD 20850
301/340-4000 Fax: 301/251-6421
News, business information, travel, shopping and financial services; shareware, CB simulation, games, and SIGs

GTE MobileNet
245 Perimeter Center Parkway
Atlanta, GA 30346
770/391-8000
Cellular service provider

Hewlett-Packard Company
Direct Marketing Organization
P. O. Box 58059
MS511L-SJ
Santa Clara, CA 95051-8059
800/HPHOME8 X 9339
Printers, scanners, OfficeJet, fax, copier

Individual Inc.
84 Sherman Street
Cambridge, MA 02140
617-354-2230
Clipping service provider

Information America
600 W. Peachtree St. NW
Atlanta, GA 30308
800/235-4008
Government and legal records

Intel Corporation
2200 Mission College Drive
Santa Clara, CA 95052-8119
408/765-8080
Microprocessors, microcomputers, and parallel computers

IBM Personal Computer Company
Route 100
Sommers,NY 10589
914/766-3700

Lexis-Nexis
9443 Springboro Pike, P.O. Box 933
Dayton, OH 45401
513/865-6800 Fax: 513/865-1350
Two full-text information services: Lexis for legal information, and Nexis for legal information

Lexmark International, Inc.
55 Railroad Avenue
Greenwich, CT 06836
800/358-5835
Lexmark Medley—Multifunction Product
Lexmark Printer—Color and Black & White

Lotus Development Corporation
55 Cambridge Pkwy
Cambridge, MA 02142
617/577-8500 Fax: 617/693-1779
Lotus Notes

MCI Mail, Telex
MCI Communications
1111 19th St. NW
Washington, DC 20036
800/444-6245
Leading e-mail network and telex carrier (MCI Mail)

Magee Enterprises, Inc.
2909 Langford Road, Suite A600
Norcross, GA 30071-1506
404/446-6611

Microsoft Corporation
One Microsoft Way
Box 97017
Redmond, WA 98052-6399
206/882-8080
Software manufacturer

Motorola Inc.
1303 E Algonquin Road
Schaumburg, IL 60196
708/576-5000
Semiconductor, telecommunication, and computer products

NACOMEX
National Computer Exchange, Inc.
118 E. 25 St., 10th Fl.
New York, NY 10010-2915
212/614-0700 Fax: 212/777-1290
Online listing and trading of used computers

NEC Technologies
1414 Massachusetts Avenue
Boxborough, MA 01719
508/264-8000

NetCom On-Line Communications Services Inc.
4000 Moorpark Avenue #209
San Jose, CA 95117
800/501-8649
TCO/IP network and Internet services

NeoSoft
1770 St. James Place, Suite 500
Houston, TX 77056
713/968-5800
Internet address: www.neosoft.com

NetScape Communications Corporation
501 E. Middlefield Road
Mountain View, CA 94043
415/254-1900

New Vision Technologies Inc.
38 Auriga Drive, Unit 13
Nepean, Ontario K2E 9A5 Canada
613/727-8184

NewsNet
NewsNet Inc.
945 Haverford Rd.
Bryn Mawr, PA 19010
215/527-8030 Fax: 215/527-0338
Online text for over 550 industry newsletters and wire
services on companies, products, technologies, and trends

Nokia
2300 Valley View Lane, Suite 100
Irving, TX 75067
214/255-8053
Nokia mobile phones and monitors

Novell Applications Group
122 E 1700 South
Provo, UT 84606-6194
801/429-7000
GroupWise and WordPerfect software

Novell Inc.
122 E 1700 South
Provo, UT 84606-6194
801/429-7000
LAN operating systems and NetWare software

OAG Electronic Edition Travel Service
Official Airline Guides, Inc.
2000 Clearwater Dr.
Oak Brook, IL 60521
708/574-6000
Reservations and flight schedules for over 600 airlines

ORBIT Search Service
Maxwell Online
8000 Westpark Dr.
McLean, VA 22102
703/442-0900 Fax: 703/893-4632
Online patent information and key references in science
and technology

PC MagNet
Ziff-Davis Publishing Company
One Park Ave.
New York, NY 10016
800/848-8990 Fax: 212/503-5519
Online text of PC Magazine and others, company data-
base, product database (50,000), and interaction with PC
Magazine editors

PageNet
4965 Preston Park Blvd.
Plano, TX 75093
214/985-4100
VoiceNow Pagers

Panasonic Communications & Systems Company
2 Panasonic Way
Secaucus, NJ 07094
201/348-7000
PCs, printers, scanners, monitors, and optical mass storage

People's Exchange
US Information Services
48 N. Gaston Ave.
Somerville, NJ 08876
908/685-1900
Electronic classified and advertising service

Portal Online
Portal Communications Co.
20863 Stevens Creek Blvd., Ste. 250
Cupertino, CA 95014
408/725-0561
Communications services such as e-mail, conferencing, meetings, chats, and access to public domain libraries

Primax
521 Almanor Avenue
Sunnyvale, CA 94086
800/338-3693
DataPen™ scanner

PRODIGY Interactive Personal Service
Prodigy Services Company
445 Hamilton Ave.
White Plains, NY 10601
914/993-8000
A broad range of services for PC users, including news, e-mail, education, shopping, banking, and travel reservations

Quik-Comm
General Electric Information Services
401 N. Washington St.
Rockville, MD 20850
301/340-4000 Fax: 301/251-6451
E-mail services, including foreign languages

Reuter's Information Services
Reuter
2 First Canadian Place, Exchange Tower, Ste. 1900
Toronto, M5X 1E3, Canada
416/364-5361 Fax: 416/364-2910
Databases and news from over 1500 sources worldwide e-mail

Sony
2720 McKeige Drive
Nashville, TN 37214
615/883-4796
MagicLink

Sprint Mail
Spring Int'l.
12490 Sunrise Valley Dr.
Reston, VA 22096
703/689-6000
Provides e-mail and telex services worldwide

T/Maker Company
1390 Villa Street
Mountain View, CA 94041
415/962-0195 Fax: 415/962-0201

Tektronix
266000 SW Parkway
Wilsonville, OR 97070-1000
503/685-3150
Printers, scanners

TelePath
M&T Publishing Inc.
411 Borel Ave., Ste. 100
San Mateo, CA 94402
415/358-9500
Technical information such as databases, languages, and
LANs

Telescan
Telescan, Inc.
10550 Richmond Ave., Ste. 250
Houston, TX 77042
713/952-1060
Information on public companies, mutual funds, and eq-
uity indexes

Visioneer
2860 W Bayshore Road
Palo Alto, CA 94303
415/812-6400
PaperPort scanner

Wynd Communications Corporation
4251 South Higuera
San Luis Obispo, CA 93401
805/541-6316 Fax: 805/547-6464
800/549-6000

Ziff Net
Ziff Communications
One Park Ave.
New York, NY 10016
800/635-6225
News and product information for PC users

GLOSSARY

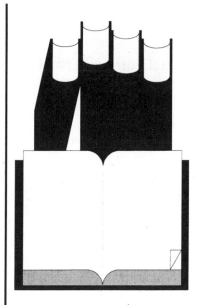

Acronyms—A word formed from the first letters of several words. Another name for shorthand commonly used in e-mail messages (e.g., ROFL means rolling on floor laughing).

Administrivia—The practice of moving piles of paper from one side of your desk to another; of attending meetings to plan your next plan; of writing memos, follow-up letters, and nonsensical status reports.

Applications—An application is an executable program that is not part of the operating system. Applications perform useful functions like manipulating data, such as a word processor or spreadsheet file.

Application Programming Interface (API)—A computer program or programs providing access between two applications. For example MAPI is Microsoft's interface between Windows applications and Microsoft Mail. The interface allows users to attach Microsoft Word documents or Excel Spreadsheets to an e-mail message or note.

Asynchronous Transfer Mode (ATM)—An emerging networking standard intended to encompass voice, video and data over fiber optic links.

Bulletin Board System (BBS)—Public forum where information is shared. You can both receive and publish data.

CD-ROM (Compact DiskRead-Only-Memory)—An optical disk from which information may be read from but not written to.

Client/Server—One or more servers that acts as a network resource manager (server) or traffic cop for the personal computer or workstation (client).

Computer literacy—The ability to use a desktop computer without fear of making a mistake. You know how to turn the machine on and off; you can select an application such as word processing or a spreadsheet from a menu by pressing a function key and you have been trained to use the applications. You are really literate if you can use DOS commands, navigate between directories and subdirectories, copy, move, or delete files, or select and use folders, files, and applications with a mouse.

Coordination intensive systems—Applications that allow work groups to increase their productivity by increasing coordination within and among corporations.

Directory—A logical segment of a disk that is used to group and logically arrange files. Directories may contain files or other directories.

Document—Any information created in an application that you type, edit, view, or save and that is stored as a file on a disk (e.g., a letter, spreadsheet, business report, or picture).

Document image processing (DIP)—Software that stores, manages, and retrieves documents as computer images. They provide image compression, scanning, printing, and retrieving to eliminate the use of photocopies. They are most useful when integrated into a local area network that provides shared access to input-output devices like scanners, laser printers, databases, and optical disks.

Downsizing—A name given to restructuring a corporation or business that is giving less control to the mainframe system or completely eliminating its mainframe capabilities and moving computer applications to a smaller, less expensive hardware platform, as a microprocessor-based server.

Dynamic Data Exchange (DDE)—The ability to take data created by one application and use it in another.

E-mail systems—An electronic mail system application for interaction between computers within an organization as well as outside sources. CompuServe is an example of an e-mail system.

Edutainment—Software that entertains as well as educates.

Electronic checkout scanner—A device used in grocery, department, and discount stores that scans the product code or price tag and enters the price in the register and records depletion of inventory.

Electronic coordination tools—These include the tools we described in this book such as fax, e-mail, and video conferencing.

Electronic Data Interchange (EDI)—The broad classification of electronic information that is shared between two separate corporations such as an automobile manufacturer and its suppliers. By using the same electronic forms and codes, the two entities can exchange information about inventories, prices, billing, and payments.

Emoticons—Specially contrived symbols that are supposed to resemble a facial expression. Unlike e-mail acronyms, which are easy to figure out, emoticons need to be read by turning your paper clockwise and reading from the right side of your page (e.g., **:-D** means I am laughing, **L:)** means I just graduated).

Facsimile machines (fax)—A device that transmits images over telephone lines.

Fax gateways—A computer or adapter board that transfers facsimile over a network.

Fax/Modem—A computer board or external unit that sends and receives facsimile information that can be transferred to or from a computer and read on the screen.

FTP (File Transfer Protocol)—A method or set of rules that lets people exchange files over networks.

Flaming—A heated reply to an electronic mail message.

HTML (Hypertext markup language)—A standard convention for designing text that appears on Internet World Wide Web pages.

Icons—The name given to little pictures or symbols located at the top of your screen that represent ideas or processes and simplify commands by eliminating keystrokes. You can point or click on the icon to accomplish the command (e.g., printer, open file, etc.).

Integrated Services Digital Networks (ISDN)—A planned worldwide telecommunications service that will use digital transmission and switching technology to support voice and digital data communication.

International Standards Organization (ISO)—Voluntary, nongovernmental organization whose members designate standards or protocols for information exchange for participating nations and nonvoting observer organizations.

IRC (Internet Relay Chat)—The ability to send keyboard messages across the Internet in real time.

LAN administrators—People responsible to maintain and protect the network/server to insure it stays up and provides uninterrupted service.

Local area networks (LANs)—A group of computers in close proximity that are connected so they can communicate with one another and share applications, data, and peripheral devices.

Mail Application Programming Interface (MAPI)—Microsoft's e-mail interface to Windows applications, which allows information created with Windows applications, such as Word or Excel, to be attached to an e-mail message.

Mainframe—A large scale (usually proprietary) computer designed to serve the needs of hundreds of users. They are typically large, centrally located machines that can be quite expensive to operate.

Message-Handling Service (MHS)—An application that takes a proprietary e-mail message and encloses it in an "envelope" with routing and header information.

Microcomputer—Any small desktop, laptop, or handheld computer using very large scale integration (VLSI) technology for manufacturing its components such as the CPU, RAM, disk controller, and serial and parallel interface electronics.

Microprocessor—A microprocessor is the computational engine for a computer. An integrated circuit that contains an Arithmetic Logic Unit (ALU), a Memory Management Unit (MMU), and a Central Processing Unit (CPU).

Modems—An electronic device used to translate digital data into analog signal capable of being transmitted over telephone lines; derived from Modulator-Demodulator.

Network operating systems (NOS)—A software program that allows interconnected computers to communicate and share resources (such as printers), data, and applications.

Object Linking and Embedding (OLE)–A feature that lets you add or "embed" data from one application (called the *server* application) into another application (called the *client* application). The embedded data may be updated directly from the *client* application by opening the *server* application from within the *client* application, making the changes to the embedded data, and then returning to what you were doing in the *client* application. This embedded data is also still "linked" to the original file (*source* file) created by the *server* application in that if the corresponding data in the original file is changed, the embedded data (*destination* file) also will change so that there is no need to update it as well. The reverse is also true for when the embedded data is changed because you are in actuality changing the *source* file.

Open Collaboration Environment (OCE)—This is an Apple Corporation standard for an applications program interfacing to the Apple Macintosh operating system.

Optical Character Recognition (OCR)—This is a technology that uses light to read and record printed characters for use in data processing. Grocery stores use OCR readers to read the Unit Product Code assigned to each food item (except loose fruits, vegetables, and nuts, of course). The checkout counters use a form of OCR that uses laser technology.

Pads—Envisioned as throwaway computers, the prototypes have two microprocessors and are a cross between a laptop and a palmtop computer. They are used like scrap paper where you may use one pad for each separate task or project and write information into the diary or calendar or daily schedule.

Palmtop computer—A small hand-held computer that weighs about a pound, is only about 4 X 6 inches in size, and usually runs off a regular AA battery. This small size and portability generally makes up for the inconvenience of not having a full-size keyboard, which becomes tedious for entering more than a few lines of data at a time.

Peer-to-Peer—A network where every PC or workstation has an equal connection to the others and a server is not necessary.

Personal Digital Assistants (PDAs)—A book-sized electronic communications device with a 5 X 4 inch video screen that can download information off your computer at home or work. It can send, receive, and sort messages, and keep a schedule and address book.

Ping—The process by which a node on a network sends out requests to another node until a response is received or the interaction between two nodes where packets of information are exchanged in response to each other's requests.

POTS (Plain Old Telephone System)—Your existing telephone lines.

PROFS (PRofessional OFfice System)—An early electronic mail system that runs on large IBM computer mainframes.

RadioMail—A company marketing and selling the Viking Express wireless electronic mail package.

Random Access Memory (RAM)—The internal memory used by the computer for data and program storage.

Retail coordination systems—Software and procedures used to coordinate sales among retail stores. They may be training materials or even demonstrations presented over teleconferencing systems.

Scanners—Any of several devices used to scan written material and convert it to an electronic readable form, e.g., digital data that can be processed by a computer.

Shareware—Software programs, games, and documents available on public networks and bulletin board systems. Shareware usually authorizes you to try the software and if you plan to continue to use it on your computer, you are asked to send a small fee, e.g., $20 to $40, for a license and documentation.

Smart phone systems—Telephones that are programmed to receive and forward voice messages when the person called is not available to answer his or her phone.

Subdirectory—A directory one or more levels below another directory in the directory structure.

Tabs—Proposed, tiny, inch-scale computers that will serve as personal communications centers for people by broadcasting the identity and location of its wearer that will enable calls to be forwarded directly to the badge wearer. The tab also should be able to trigger automatic door locks and accept notes, instructions, or other forms of input from people anywhere in the building by using radio transceivers that link tabs and other mobile computers to the wired network.

Tape backup system—A combination of hardware (tape drive) and software that can be used to store files from a microcomputer such as a LAN server and provides a backup of the users' files in case the LAN's disk drive fails for any reason.

Technophobe—A person who knows little about technology and is sometimes afraid of it.

Teleconferencing—Synonymous with video conferencing. It includes a television graphics and audio system that allows people to hold conferences in geographically separated facilities or for instructors to conduct classes in several locations at the same time.

Telecommuter—An employee or contract worker works out of their home and communicates via computers with their bosses and associates.

Total Quality Management (TQM)—A management approach that examines and improves work process flow to achieve higher employee productivity and teamwork, often involving customers and enhanced quality of products and services.

URL (Uniform Resource Locator)—An address on the Internet.

USENET (User Network)—An informal or formal computer bulletin board.

Video transceivers—Devices that send and receive video or compressed video signals.

Voice annotation–The ability to add voice to an e-mail message or other computer screen.

Wide Area Network (WAN)—A group of computers that are connected so they can communicate and share applications, data, and peripheral devices. Wide Area Networks may span states, countries, or continents.

Wireless communicating device—A radio modem that sends and receives switched-packet radio messages such as e-mail via satellite to designated addresses.

Wireless messaging units—The individual message packets of 512- or 1000-byte (character) message units sent and received on a wireless network.

Wireless network—The system that sends, stores, and receives switched-packet radio signals. It includes the modem transceiver tied to a laptop or hand-held computer, software to handle the communications transmission and reception, and a sophisticated communications system that transmits and receives the users' messages via 900MHz radio signals routed through an earth satellite.

Workgroup—The collection of people that you interact with on the job.

Workstation—A microcomputer attached to a network and used to perform user tasks.

2s

0585

HD
30.2
C87
1996

WITHDRAWN
From Library Collection

WITHDRAWN
From Library Collection

Reinsch Library
Marymount University
2807 North Glebe Road
Arlington, Virginia 22207